MW00512378

Intermittent Fasting

The complete guide for beginners

Author

Kim J. Forte

© Copyright 2020- Kim J. Forte

-All rights reserved.

The content contained within this book may not be reproduced, duplicated or transmitted without direct written permission from the author or the publisher.

Under no circumstances will any blame or legal responsibility be held against the publisher, or author, for any damages, reparation, or monetary loss due to the information contained within this book, either directly or indirectly.

Legal Notice:

This book is copyright protected. It is only for personal use. You cannot amend, distribute, sell, use, quote or paraphrase any part, or the content within this book, without the consent of the author or publisher.

Disclaimer Notice:

Please note the information contained within this document is for educational and entertainment purposes only. All effort has been executed to present accurate, up to date, reliable, complete information. No warranties of any kind are declared or implied. Readers acknowledge that the author is not engaging in the rendering of legal, financial, medical or professional advice. The content within this book has been derived from various sources. Please consult a licensed professional before attempting any techniques outlined in this book.

By reading this document, the reader agrees that under no circumstances is the author responsible for any losses, direct or indirect, that are incurred as a result of the use of information contained within this document, including, but not limited to, errors, omissions, or inaccuracies.

TABLE OF CONTENTS

Introduction

Chapter 01

    Basics of Intermittent Fasting

    Why it Works

    Fits your life

    Caloric restriction

    Changes your physiology

    Fasting is for...Everyone?

Chapter 02

    Myths of Intermittent Fasting

    Myth #1: Fasting is the Same as Starvation

    Myth #2: Fasting will Make You Gain Weight

    Myth #3: Fasting is not Sustainable Long-term

    Myth #4: Fasting Causes you to Binge

    Myth #5: You Can Eat Whatever You Want

    Myth #6: You'll be Constantly Hungry

Chapter 03

    Benefits and Risks

    Benefits of Intermittent Fasting

    Weight loss

    Risks of Intermittent Fasting

Chapter 04

    Styles of Intermittent Fasting

    14/10 Method

    5:2 Method

    24 Hour

    The Warrior Diet

    The Warrior Diet might work in theory, but it will

    Alternate Day

Chapter 05

    Transitioning into Intermittent Fasting

    Transitioning into 14:10

    Early Eating Schedule

    Mid-day Eating Schedule

    Evening Eating Schedule

    Transitioning into 5:2

Monday and Thursday fasting days

Wednesday and Saturday fasting days

Transitioning into 24 Hour Fast

What to Eat to Break your Fast

Transitioning into the Warrior Diet

Early eating schedule

Mid-day eating schedule

Evening eating schedule

Transitioning into Alternate Day Fasting

Chapter 06

Intermittent Fasting and Your Diet

5:2 Method and Alternate Day: Calorie Restriction

Breakfast ideas

Lunch and dinner ideas

Snacking ideas

Warrior Diet: Paleo

Breakfast ideas

Lunch and dinner ideas

Maintaining Well-Balanced Meals

Breakfast ideas

Here are some lunch ideas

Dinner ideas

Chapter 07

Motivation to Stick with Your Plan

Distract Yourself

Remind Yourself of Your Goals

Be Compassionate Towards Yourself

Get Some Support + Bonus 16/8 method

Chapter 08: Chapter bonus: Fasting

Overview of the 16/8 Method

Why It Works

Caloric Restriction

Who Shouldn't Try It?

Pregnant Women

People with Medical and Mental Illness

Other Mental Illness

Advanced Diabetes

Irritable Bowel Syndrome

Children

Chapter 09

Following the 16/8 Method Step-by-Step

Starting from Scratch: Transitioning from No Fast to Fasting

Step 1: Making a Goal

Step 2: Planning Your Eating Schedule (and Your Sleeping Schedule!)

Step 3: Planning Your Meals

Step 4: Taking a Before Picture

Step 5: Sleeping Well the Night before You Start

Step 6: Starting the Transition

Step 7: Preparing Yourself for Magic . . . and Discomfort

Step 8: Recording Your Progress

Starting from Previous Fast: Transitioning from the Different Types

Step 1: Planning Your Eating Schedule

Step 2: Starting Your Transition

Step 3: Preparing for Discomfort

Step 4: Recording Things in Your Journal

Typical Schedule for the 16/8 method

Early Eating Schedule

Midday Eating Schedule

Evening Eating Schedule

Chapter 10

Combining Specific Diets and Intermittent Fasting

Keto

Calorie Restriction

Benefits and Risks

Chapter 11

Sample Menus for Intermittent Fasting

What to Eat First Thing in the Morning What
to Eat at the End of Your Eating Window?

Fasting with Basic Nutritional Guidelines

Well-Balanced Breakfast Ideas

Well-Balanced Lunch Ideas

Well-Balanced Dinner Ideas

Here are some meal ideas

Side Notes

Fasting with Keto

Keto Breakfast Ideas

Keto Lunch Ideas

Keto Dinner Ideas

Fasting with Caloric Restriction

Low-Calorie Breakfast Ideas

Low-Calorie Lunch Ideas

Low-Calorie Dinner Ideas

Low-Calorie Foods to Choose From

Chapter 12

Exercise and Fasting

When to Exercise

Exercising before You Eat

Exercising after You Eat

Go with What Makes You Comfortable

Exercising on Different Fasting Schedules

Chapter 13

Troubleshooting Difficulties while Fasting

The Struggle

Weight Gain

Keeping a Journal of Progress

Mindfulness

Support Systems

Conclusion

Introduction

Fasting has been around for millennia. It has played important roles in religious and medical literature for nearly as long. In many modern religions, fasting is the way to create spiritual connection, to find guidance or to improve mindfulness. Fasts that automatically come to mind are Lent in Catholicism and Orthodox Christianity, Ramadan in Islam or meditation fasts is some Buddhist schools. Lent lasts 40 days, and while some churches may allow more freedom with the fast, traditionally Lent required a fast where only one meal a day was eaten. During Ramadan, a month long fast, Muslims don't eat while the sun is up and then eat once the sun is down. Essentially, it is an eight to 12 hour fast, with some time to eat at night and early in the morning. In some Buddhist schools, fasting takes place to aid in meditation and spiritual practices. This often happens every day, with the dinner meal skipped.

So, within religions and spiritual practices, there are many different kinds of fasts.

People have also fasted for political reasons. Perhaps most famously is Gandhi and his social protests. He fasted multiple times to protest a variety of social issues in India. There have been other hunger strikes throughout history, where people fasted to create political change including suffragette fasting in Europe and the U.S. Many political fasts promote a feeling of guilt in those watching, and can result in change, though it has often resulted in death as well.

Medically, fasting has been around since the time of Hippocrates. Fasting was prescribed during times when the patient was sick enough that eating was considered detrimental. Past physicians believed that fasting would help with the healing of injuries and diseases. While it's unclear whether this was actually true, today, modern fasting is associated with better health improvements. In fact, intermittent fasting is our modern take on fasting for healing.

Intermittent fasting is when you choose not to eat for a specific amount of time. For example, you might fast during the evening and night hours, or you might fast every other day. In general, intermittent fasting doesn't go beyond a day of fasting. So, you won't see many intermittent fasts that are 30 hours of fasting or longer. Despite how it may sound, intermittent fasting is not starvation and in fact, it's quite healthy. Intermittent fasts are about improving your health. In general, it can benefit people who are looking to lose weight, improve their blood sugar levels, and reduce their insulin resistance.

In this book, we'll cover the basics of intermittent fasting. We'll explore the different kinds, from the everyday ease of the 14/10 method to the difficult but rewarding alternate-day fast. We'll also discuss who is a perfect candidate for trying intermittent fasting, and who should refrain from it. We'll go over the benefits and risks, and explore associated research studies that demonstrate the effectiveness of intermittent fasting. Finally, we'll go into detail about schedules and possible menus for starting intermittent fasting. With this book, you'll get a thorough introduction to intermittent fasting and you'll begin your journey to starting your own intermittent fast. Let's begin.

Chapter 01

Basics of Intermittent Fasting

The beauty of social media is that ideas can be shared around the world and gain popularity very quickly. It's probably why you're here, reading this book. On social media you can find many influencers and celebrities who have tried intermittent fasting, and wholeheartedly advocate for it. Whether you want to look like the actors who play superheroes or whether you just want to get healthier, intermittent fasting can help you achieve your goals.

In the introduction, we covered how fasting was used throughout history for health, political, religious reasons. Some of these fasts are very similar to intermittent fasting. In general, intermittent fasting is when you time your eating to fit within a specific window during your day or week. Your fasting hours might just be during the night, or they might extend to a full 24 hours. When comparing intermittent fasting to religious fasting, you will see some similarities with Ramadan and Lent. During Ramadan, most people don't eat during the day, and instead eat all their meals at night. This is very similar to a 16/8 fast or even a 20/4 fast, where eating takes place in a small eight- or four-hour window at night. Depending on the style of Lent a person follows, you may only have one large meal in the day instead of many meals. Or you may only eat for some portion of the week and fast completely on other days. This can also be quite like intermittent fasting schedules. The difference between religious fasts and intermittent fasting are, of course, the purpose but also the timing. Religious fasts often take place for a short period of time like 20-40 days, but intermittent fasting can be a whole lifestyle change, and result in you fasting for years! It's not necessary to do it for the long term, but many people continue it even when they meet their goals for fasting.

There are so many different varieties of intermittent fasting that you'll have and easy way of finding one that fits into your lifestyle. In general, there are the methods that require you to eat in a small window every day. These are the methods like the 12/12, 14/10, 16/8, and 20/4. In these methods, the first number is how many hours you fast, and the second number is how many hours are in your eating window. You would eat all your meals during that window of time, and during the fasting point, you would just drink liquids.

The other types of fasts are those that include 24 hours of fasting between eating days. Some of these do calorie restricted meals during the fasting period so that hunger doesn't become overwhelming. Methods that do the longer 24 hours fast (with or without small meals on fasting days) include alternate day fasts, the 5:2 fast, and a general 24 hour fast. Alternate day fasts and 5:2 fasts can be similar as they take place during the course of one week. However, alternate day fasts require fasting three or four days of the week, alternating your eating days and your fasting days. While the 5:2 fast is eating normally for five days with two days of fasting spread out within the week. The 24 hours fast is one you might do once a week or even just once a month! Whichever fast you choose to do, you'll want to choose one that fits your daily life. We'll discuss these kinds of fasts later in the book.

It's important to mention that intermittent fasting isn't a diet. While people use it to receive health benefits (like they do for dieting), intermittent fasting isn't a diet at all. Most diets are focused on what you eat, however, intermittent fasting is all about when you eat. It focuses on the timing of eating to change your body's current state and bring it more into homeostasis. This can sound a little fantasy-like. Afterall, how can changing the times you eat help? Well, there's a lot of research out there about intermittent fasting, and depending on the type of fasting you follow, intermittent fasting can change your metabolism, insulin levels, and more. Let's explore more about why intermittent fasting works.

Why it Works

I can tell you that you'll lose weight on intermittent fasting and you'll become healthier. But none of that explains why? Why does fasting have such positive reviews and a following? Intermittent fasting works for so many reasons, but the main ones are the fact that it can fit in your daily life, changes some of your physiology, and can result in some caloric restriction.

Fits your life

Diets cause a lot of changes in your life. They often require specific foods that must be eaten. This can be frustrating if you live in an area where some foods aren't available. It can also be frustrating cost wise, as a lot of diet foods can be quite expensive. All of these can impact your motivation to continue dieting. Intermittent fasting doesn't cause this change to your life. You don't have to eat specific types of food when fasting. Nor do you have to spend a fortune following the schedule. All it requires of you is to eat at a specific time of day, and eat healthy meals during your eating window. This can ease the strain of starting a new fasting schedule. This also means that you won't have to do a huge change to your lifestyle.

Cravings can be a nightmare when following other styles of dieting. You can follow a low-calorie diet, but you'll probably miss eating that burger from your favorite shop, or having a scoop of ice cream with your kids. You could follow a very low or no carb diet, but you might end up missing bread, and feel a lot of restrictions when it comes to choosing your food. This can reduce the sustainability of dieting in your life. Intermittent fasting can be more reliable because you're not going to have any cravings. It doesn't restrict what you eat, which is honestly the hardest part of most conventional diets. By not restricting what you eat, you're not likely to struggle with cravings. Depending on which fasting method you choose, you might struggle with hunger, but probably not cravings.

Many of us don't follow a set eating schedule. We will often find ourselves skipping meals when we get into the flow of work or when we oversleep. Because we don't have set times to eat normally, it's really easy to change our schedule at the drop of a hat. That's why some intermittent fasts can fit into your daily schedule. If you only have to shift your eating a bit during the day, you will not struggle with the change so much. For example, if you choose to follow the 14/10 fasting schedule, you'll only have to shift your breakfast and dinner times by a couple of hours. That's so easy! Other methods of fasting can be easier, or harder depending on your current lifestyle.

Intermittent fasting doesn't require a huge shift in how you eat, unlike some other diets, which is why it can be easier to follow and fit your lifestyle better than conventional (or unconventional) diets.

Caloric restriction

Another reason that fasting works is because it can result in some unplanned calorie restriction. Calorie restriction is one of the reasons people lose weight in a regular low-calorie diet. Unplanned calorie restriction means that you have a slightly lower number of daily or weekly calories than you normally eat during the day or week. Normally, an adult who is of average height and weight, eats between 2000-2200 calories a day. When fasting, you might have difficulty eating as much as you normally do during the day. Afterall, you only have a small eating window in some fasting methods. So, you may end up eating 1800 calories a day. This is a significant reduction in calories, and it's all unplanned. By having this reduction, you're guaranteed to lose some weight while fasting.

In some methods of fasting, you might have some planned caloric restriction. The 24-hour methods which result in 24 hours without food, obviously result in significant weekly calorie reductions. If a healthy adult of average height and weight eats 14,000 - 15,400 calories per week, then by having some 24-hour fasts can reduce that by 2,000-6,000 calories, depending on the type of fast you choose. Alternate day fasting will provide you with way more calorie reductions than other fasts. Again, all of this reduction will result in weight loss. Because some fasts can be easier than following a consistent calorie reduction diet, fasting for this purpose can give you some good results without causing a lot of pain.

Changes your physiology

This one is a little complicated and will be discussed extensively in the chapter on benefits and risks. However, to give you a basic overview, intermittent fasting works because it can change some of your physiology and put your body back to homeostasis. By shifting your eating times, you force your body to change the way it uses its stores of glucose. This results in your body shifting from burning glucose as fuel to burning fat because the glucose stores have been used up during the fasting window. This leads to a whole host of health benefits. The best part is that these health benefits continue even after you're back to eating during your eating window. Fasting can also change your hormone levels, which also help your health and can provide so many benefits, especially to those who are already struggling with health issues. We'll cover all of this more in the chapter on benefits and risks.

Fasting is for...Everyone?

Intermittent fasting can sound rather fantastic and easy. But don't let its simple description fool you. It's a process and it can be difficult to stick with. Because of this, it's important to consider fasting carefully before you try it. Despite how much I wish I could say that fasting is for everyone, this simply isn't true. Fasting works for some, and for others it can be a dangerous affair. Here are some people who should and who should not try intermittent fasting. As always, please follow your doctor's recommendation about intermittent fasting before starting. Let's say you already live a pretty healthy life. You exercise regularly, eat healthy meals, and are generally untroubled by any illnesses, mental or physical. If this describes you, then you could go ahead and try your fasting method of choice. You probably wouldn't have many or any side effects because you already know the basics of doing the best for your body. However, if you're like the rest of us, who have lived off fast food for most of our lives and are looking for a change, you should consider your general health and discipline towards a fast before starting. Whatever your current health status is, there are some things you should consider before starting a fast.

Consider your social priorities before you start fasting. Many people enjoy meals with their friends and family on the weekends. We also tend to eat meals with our children in the evenings. So, once you've chosen a method you're interested in, you'll need to consider how you are going to schedule your meals to fit your social engagements. If you're doing a daily fast with a method like 14/10 or 20/4, think about when you'll end your fast. Also consider if your family will be following your pattern, or if you'll be going it alone. If you're the one cooking for your family, will you be able to handle any cravings that come from watching them eat while you don't? Essentially, just consider the impact on your day to day eating habits. This will help you narrow down types of fasting that will work for you. Beyond the social considerations, you'll have to consider your support system. It's really empowering to have people cheering for you when you're doing something hard, or new. Think about going to college and having a support system. It's so much easier than going alone. Fasting can be very difficult, and while you can go it alone, it's easier with a support system in place. This is especially true if you're planning on this being a lifestyle change.

So, go through your phone contacts, and pick a few people who are reliable and can offer you support and encouragement while you start your fast. These are the people who won't make you feel guilty about not eating when they eat. They're the people who will encourage you when all you want to do is eat cake at midnight during your fasting hours. They're the people who may even choose to fast with you! Just have a support system. Furthermore, if you don't have a support system in your daily life, create your own support system by becoming active in online support groups and health coaching groups.

This is a more practical consideration but think about how your emotions might change as you fast. The first change in your eating schedule can lead to some changed moods. You might even have a change in your sleeping habits. These changes, though different, are related and can affect your life. You might be tired at work and being tired makes you feel very hungry. You may have feelings of anger when you're hungry (commonly known as being 'hangry'). You may have other shifts in your mood, but it's different for everyone. You'll need to make plans for adapting to your body's changes before starting your fast. This will help your adjustment period.

One final consideration is for anyone who does a lot of exercise or workouts. You can exercise while on your fast, but you'll need to be slow and careful when transitioning into your fast. You'll probably have to change how much protein and fiber you eat. You'll also need to plan your exercising window to coincide with your eating window. You don't want to exercise and then fast for 10 hours. Instead, you want to make sure that you have a meal after you exercise so that your body can recover. If you're an athlete, you're going to want to talk with your doctor to see if intermittent fasting will be beneficial for you before starting.

While it's important to take all of these things into consideration, fasting still isn't helpful for everyone. Here are people who shouldn't be fasting:

- Those who are pregnant or want to be pregnant.

- Those who have experienced eating disorders, anxiety, or depression (not without a doctor's recommendation).

- Those who have some medical illnesses (again, not without a doctor's recommendation).

- Those who are children. Seriously. Anyone under the age of 18 probably shouldn't fast.

Let's look at these demographics in detail to explain why fasting won't work for people in them. Pregnancy is possibly one of the only times in your life when you can eat whatever you want, and people won't stop you. That might not be healthy though, so it's easy to see how you may want to lose weight while pregnant. But fasting is not the way to go. Being pregnant means that you are providing the necessary nutrition for both you and your baby. Your baby's development depends entirely on what you put in your body. Fasting will result in you not intaking the right amount of food for both of you. This can negatively affect your child's development. Just like how drinking alcohol or smoking while pregnant can result in detrimental fetal development, so too can fasting. If your heart is set on trying intermittent fasting, then please try it after your baby has been weaned and you're both healthy.

If you're trying to get pregnant, then don't do intermittent fasting. There has been a couple animal studies with intermittent fasting that resulted in females having changed menstruation, low fertility, and skipped periods. While this research hasn't been carried over to humans, you don't really want to take the risk. So, wait to start intermittent fasting until another time in your life.

Intermittent fasting can mess around with your hormones. It will shift your mood at the beginning. This can be dangerous for those who already struggle with mental illnesses or past mental illnesses. Fasting can push you into a relapse of anxiety or depression because of the change in your hormone levels. If you've experienced anxiety or depression before, you should talk to your doctor before trying fasting. You should also set up checks with your support system so they can identify if you're becoming more anxious or depressed while on a fast.

If you have ever had an eating disorder, you shouldn't fast at all. Eating disorders are all about having a really bad relationship with food, and even if you've recovered, fasting can push you back into disordered eating.

Anorexia, bulimia, and binge eating are all different kinds of disordered eating. Doing a fast while experiencing one of these disorders, or after recovering from one, can push you back into disordered eating. It's easy to start fasting and then just keep going without enough eating windows if you've already experienced anorexia. Fasting could also cause a flare in binge eating when breaking your fast because you're hungry from not eating for several hours. Both these situations are dangerous for your body and your mental state. So if you have experienced an eating disorder, fasting is not recommended at all, not even with a doctor's recommendation. Please don't endanger your mental health just to try and improve your physical health.

Intermittent fasting can have some good benefits for your body. If you are already struggling with some medical issues, you need to take a moment to step back and reassess your fasting ideas. Fasting can help with insulin resistance, so if you're prediabetic or even have been recently diagnosed with type 2 diabetes, intermittent fasting can help you, though your doctor should discuss it with you first. However, if you have been diagnosed with diabetes for a while, and have already experienced significant damage from it, then intermittent fasting shouldn't be pursued. The reason being that fasting changes your metabolic rate, insulin levels, and blood-sugar levels. If you're already struggling with maintaining these things, then fasting will throw you for a loop. Talk to your doctor if you're concerned about your weight, and they can give you some good advice for approaching a diet change or fast. Please don't just jump right in.

While diabetes is the primary concern when approaching fasting, if you have any medical difficulties, you should really talk to your doctor. The final demographic of people who should not fast are children. There are a lot of reasons why children shouldn't fast. One of them is about people and their relationship to food. As children, we learn about food, how it makes us feel, and grow attachments to our eating habits. These habits can follow us into adulthood. Just think about it: What food brings you comfort? What do you eat when you're sad or angry? When did you learn that? A lot of this comes from childhood and what we learned during it. Comfort food literally comforts us, and the food item can be different for each person. So, what we learn about food as children can follow us. If what children learn is to restrict eating, then they're not going to learn about good relationships with food.

As they grow older, it will always be about restricting food. This can lead to another problem.

If children fast while growing, they'll learn that food should be restricted. This can create disordered eating, specifically anorexia. We've already discussed the importance of not fasting if you've experienced anorexia. But it's critical that children aren't taught restrictive eating in case they end up not eating at all. Now of course, fasting will not automatically cause anorexia. But it can be a trigger. Children have disordered eating for a lot of reasons, but it all narrows down to have an 'ideal' body type. If children think that fasting can get them there, then they may choose to go beyond fasting and into starvation. So, it's critically important that children don't fast.

To wrap up this chapter, I urge you to first talk to your doctor before fasting. This recommendation is for anyone who is unsure about how fasting will help them, or anyone who has a current health condition. Your doctor will be able to tell you definitively about whether fasting is for you or not and help ensure that you won't affect your health negatively during your fast. Fasting can benefit a lot of people, but it's not for everyone. In the next few chapters, we're going to explore more about fasting. First, we will tackle those pesky myths you've probably heard about fasting. After that, we will examine the benefits and risks of fasting, as well as the studies that support its effectiveness. Before choosing whether you want to fast or not, check out these next two chapters.

They provide some awesome information that may persuade you to try fasting.

Chapter 02
Myths of Intermittent Fasting

Myths are a beautiful thing. They're presented as absolute fact, without any proof, and we're all expected to believe them. However, they often don't have any sort of basis and can easily be debunked with just a little knowledge. This strange nature of myth can create some of our greatest stories. But in our more modern era, myths can change our beliefs and influence our decisions. Think about a lot of the myths, and often straight up lies, sent out over social media and how they negatively affect people. Myths like these can change the way we do business, take care of our families, or even approach politics or religion. The most amazing thing about myths is that we all believe them. It doesn't matter how much of a skeptic you are, there is at least one myth that you believe in. As our society keeps creating more myths, there are more and more opportunities for you to believe things that are simply untrue. This chapter is all about making sure you don't believe the myths associated with intermittent fasting.

Anytime that you have a new experience or a new idea, there are always going to be people who are willing to poke holes in it or make things up about it. I could say, "Intermittent fasting is a cure all for everything! Have appendicitis? Fast! Have a headache? Fast! Getting a little heavy while pregnant? Fast! It will solve all your problems!" And you could choose to believe me. But really, without proof you wouldn't know if I've just made these statements up or not (and yes, I did make them up, please don't fast if you're pregnant). If you choose to believe many of the other myths about fasting, then you can miss out on some great opportunities with fasting. Or worse, you could hurt yourself if you believe some of the myths. So, it's important to fact check before following believing and follow myths. While intermittent fasting is a bit new, there are still a lot of myths about it. Before starting with intermittent fasting, it's important to go through the myths so that you know exactly what is fact and what is fiction about intermittent fasting. Because we want you to believe us when we say that fasting can be beneficial, we'll include the sources for this information and research studies associated with each myth.

Myth #1: Fasting is the Same as Starvation

When many people think about fasting, they think about starvation. After all, if you're not eating, then you must be starving. However, this myth isn't true. We fast every day, for about eight hours as we sleep, and yet we don't starve. You can even skip a meal on top of your sleep time, and not starve. Beyond just this basic daily fast we all do; starvation changes our body in a different way in comparison to intermittent fasting.

In the U.S. starvation is uncommon, though it's more common to have some food insecurity. If you are experiencing starvation, you'll have not eaten for a while, or eaten very low-calorie meals for several days.

In fact, your starvation response starts after merely three days of not eating enough calories (Berg, Tymoczko, & Strye, 2002). During this time, you will lose weight, but you will also damage your body. In this case, your body and your brain know that you're starving, and they decide to try and save you. So your brain slows down your metabolism and sends out hormones to make you very hungry. Your body starts looking for food elsewhere. Now the science behind starvation is really detailed, but suffice it to say, normally our body gets its energy from our food, which increases our blood-glucose levels, and our insulin — all of which feeds our body. However, when starving, our body runs out of its stores of glucose and starts searching for other sources of energy. In the search for protein, your body will start cannibalizing itself, eating through important cells, and muscles. It's not a quick process, because your body still needs to function to find more food.

However, without food, your body will slowly lose its functionality, leading to death. Most of us won't starve to death in the U.S. Even when eating a very low-calorie diet, our body will keep pushing us to eat and with a lot of access to food, even if most is unhealthy, we're not likely to starve to death. However, we can still feel the effects of the starvation response without the right nutrition during the day. Not only will our brain keep sending out hunger warnings, but we'll also have a shift in emotions and sometimes, cognitive function. Researchers during WWII studied starvation to determine how our bodies react to it. This study is known as the Minnesota Starvation Experiment (Keys et al., 1950), and it found some interesting effects on our brains from starvation. Many of the participants experienced emotional swings, felt cognitively foggy, and had dreams about food. They became depressed, anxious, and irritable. Physically, they experienced fluctuating body temperature, felt weak, and had reduced stamina. Their heart rate also decreased. These effects were felt in a stage of semistarvation, where they were eating, but only a little every day and very little of what they ate was healthy. So even when having food, we can experience the effects of starvation.

Intermittent fasting is very different from starvation because you won't be without food for three days. In fact, so long as you're following a set, healthy, fasting schedule, you will only be without food for 24 hours or less. So, you will not to initiate your natural starvation response. Our body is used to normal fasting, eating states. Once you eat your last meal before a fast, your body has high blood-sugar levels, and increased insulin which are all fueling your body. The body also stores the extra glucose and puts it aside for later. After the first several hours, your body starts to reduce it's insulin levels and your blood-sugar levels also drop. Your liver releases it's stores of glucose and then your body starts using fatty tissue to continue fueling itself since it's blood-sugar levels are lower. This state is known as ketosis. Your body remains in this state for a while, even when you eat again (Berg, Tymoczko, & Strye, 2002). Because you're providing your body with food, even after 24 hours without, your body doesn't shift into its starvation response. Instead, it sticks with its stage of ketosis, with reduced insulin levels and blood-sugar levels, before getting more energy from your next meal.

It's important to note that while there are differences between starvation and fasting, any fast taken for too long will result in starvation. Any diet, where you are eating less than 1000 calories a day, puts you at risk for starting your body's starvation response.

However, this response won't happen immediately. So long as you are eating something during your days, you'll be ok. In most fasts, you're going to eat your regular daily calories every day. But in some fasts like the 5:2 and the Alternate Day fasting, you'll have periods of low-calorie intake. Even during these periods, you'll only be without food for 24 hours or less.

So, while doing intermittent fasting, your body shouldn't have a starvation response.

Myth #2: Fasting will Make You Gain Weight

This myth is closely related to the previous myth. It's connected to the starvation response, or as many people call it, "Starvation Mode." Starvation mode is the same thing as our starvation response, but just in a more sensationalized perspective. The general myth most people have is that fasting will put you into starvation mode, which means your metabolism slows down, you'll start hoarding all the fuel your body takes in because of the slow metabolism, and thus, you'll gain weight. Let's break this down because it's a complicated myth.

We've already covered how fasting won't put you into starvation mode if it's done correctly. So, we're going to explore the metabolism aspect. When you're starving, and your body/brain starts trying to save itself, it starts to lower it's metabolism. Your metabolism is what helps you maintain your body's weight and repair your cells. It's how your body processes the food you eat and turns it into the fuel used to power your every action. During starvation, your metabolism rate will reduce because you don't have enough food to keep it running at its optimal level. This is to conserve energy for your most important living functions. Because people often think that fasting is the same as starvation, they expect your metabolism to slow while fasting, resulting in you gaining weight. This is confusing because during starvation, yes, your metabolic rate decreases, but your body is using all the stores it has. This means that there isn't any extra fuel! You will not gain weight when you're starving. It's impossible. So, carrying that belief over to fasting, just doesn't work. In most diet culture, you'll hear people talk about 'fast' metabolism and 'slow' metabolism. Having a fast metabolism is supposed to help you lose weight because you're burning more food and fuel than you're eating and storing. A slow metabolism is supposed to make you gain weight because you're not burning enough fuel and everything extra you eat gets stored. So, when people think about this myth, they think that your lack of food, will reduce your metabolism, which will lead to more food storage, with less energy and stores being used. However, this isn't true with fasting. Fasting improves your metabolism and uses your stores of energy efficiently (Patterson et al., 2016). Done right, it's likely that you will lose weight when fasting, not gain weight.

While I'd like to fully debunk this myth, there is some truth to it, and it all comes down to diet. It's possible that you can gain weight when fasting, but it's not because of your metabolic rate. If you choose to eat regular meals that exceed your daily calories, then you're going to gain weight. This is the same with any diet, any fast, or any food you eat. If you exceed what your body will use, energy/food wise, then you'll gain weight. So, it is possible that you'll gain weight when fasting. But if you do, it's not because of a lower metabolic rate, and is more because of poorly planned diet. To prevent this, it's important that you eat well-balanced nutritious foods. This will help you maintain weight, or possibly lose some if it's a shift from your normal diet. You could also combine calorie restriction with fasting, and we'll discuss this in a later chapter. Basically, if you gain weight when fasting, then it's due to diet and you'll need to watch what you eat to lose or maintain your weight.

Myth #3: Fasting is not Sustainable Long-term

There are so many diets out there that are not sustainable. What immediately comes to mind are the types of diet where you eat only one type of food, like the cabbage soup diet. These kinds of diets are not sustainable because it's easy to start craving more types of food. Your body itself will crave the nutrients it needs, while you'll get bored with that single kind of food. A lot of diets that are fad diets aren't sustainable because they often don't provide your body with the requirements it needs to function well. This results in you being hungry and craving the foods that are prohibited in those diets. Fasting isn't like fad and doesn't restrict certain types of food. So, while you might get hungry, it's unlikely you'll have any brutal cravings. This can increase the sustainability of fasting.

Also, there are so many kinds of fasting. Some of them are really easy to incorporate into your daily life, like the 14/10 fast or the 16/8 fast. With these diets, you're simply extending your fast further than your normal eight hours of sleep. Sometimes this means eating your last meal early, or your first meal late. Because these two types are simple and easy to get into, it can be easy to maintain as well. Other types of fasting can be even easier, depending on your own personality. But the reality remains that fasting can be quickly started and maintained.

Finally, a lot of people find fasting much easier to sustain than long term calorie restriction. Long-term calorie restriction is your typical, doctor approved diet. You reduce your eaten calories by a bit every day and you lose weight. However, this can be difficult to maintain because it requires you to pick and choose what you eat carefully and can restrict social eating. In a study comparing alternate day fasting and calorie restriction, the researchers found that the participants felt the fasting was easier to sustain (Alhamdan, 2016). This has been echoed in other studies and even anecdotally. Even though hunger could be an issue with alternate day fasting, that's not always the case as participants found that their hunger on fasting days was reduced after two weeks of following the fast schedule (Klemple et al.,

2010). So, fasting can be easy to start, maintain, and sustain because it doesn't restrict you.

Intermittent fasting is considered a lifestyle change. I know this is mentioned in many different diets, but with fasting, it's the easiest way to change your eating habits. It can change your health and reduce your weight. By following it in the long-term, you'll maintain all those benefits. So, fasting is and can be sustainable.

Myth #4: Fasting Causes you to Binge

This myth is based slightly on reality. It comes from how we often react when we skip a meal. We all know the feeling. You've decided to work through lunch and by the time you get home, you are dramatically dying of hunger. You go to your pantry and start gorging on anything that will fill that empty void and end hunger. When we come to, we're surrounded by the remnants of what we've eaten. It can be very surprising how much has been eaten during a moment of, what feels like, desperate hunger.

The thing that can be doubly amazing is that during this feeling of almost insatiable hunger, our bodies are sending out signals that tell us to eat, but also to stop after a certain point. Unfortunately, most of us are incapable of hearing that, "I'm full" signal from our brains when in this state. So, we overeat. By a lot. This is a typical feeling of a binge. If we get to the point where we're very hungry, we often just start eating everything available and have a hard time stopping. So yes, it's possible that you'll binge when breaking your fast with your first meal. But it doesn't have to happen, and it doesn't happen to many people. This is because people understand how their hunger works, and how to break their fast properly to prevent binging.

When breaking your fast, you want to ease into it. Depending on what type of fast you have, you may be breaking your fast after 14 hours, or after 24 hours. So, it's important to slowly break your fast. Don't just start gorging on everything you see. Take a deep breath. Have some coffee or tea. Then start eating with something small. Take a short break, and then eat a little more. Listen for your "I'm full" signal from your body. Then stop eating.

A way that can also help with this feeling is to be more mindful while you eat. Mindfulness is a common term now a days, but it can be applied to eating. Mindfulness means that you make yourself become aware of the 'now' moment. What is happening right now? What are you seeing, hearing, tasting, feeling, and smelling? At this very moment where are you and how did you get there? All of this is taking a step back and focusing on this present moment. When following mindfulness, you are not just focused on one thing, but also allowing your thoughts to come and go without you evaluating them or judging yourself. But what does this have to do with eating and binging?

Mindfulness and eating can go hand in hand. Essentially, you want to look at your current present moment, but also being aware of your body's reaction as you eat. It means eating slowly, tasting each piece of food you put in your mouth, and slowly savoring it. You could focus on your five senses while you eat and say exactly what each of them is feeling. It's also about listening to your body's reaction and looking for that full signal. Being aware of our body and how we're filling up can help us ensure that we're not giving into the hunger monster.

With mindfulness in your toolkit, you can learn what the full feeling means to your body. You can learn when to slow down and to stop eating. This can take some time. We often bypass the full feeling, so don't stress yourself as it will take time for you to get used to it. It can come along much earlier than you may have felt before, but if you can remain mindful while you eat, you can reduce the likelihood of binging. Be mindful as you eat so that you're paying attention to your hunger signals. All these things can help you break your fast without binging. So, there is some truth to this myth, but it's easily managed and prevented.

Myth #5: You Can Eat Whatever You Want

With most intermittent fasting methods, you don't have to restrict your diet when you have your eating window. This isn't in all methods, just some. The myth that you can eat whatever you want comes from this unrestriction on what you're eating. Much like the myth before this one, there is some truth to this. While fasting, you still eat whatever you want, but solely in your eating window. If you want to eat fast food every single day during your eating window, then go ahead. But...it's very likely that fasting won't help you in this case. If you're eating unhealthy foods, you're likely consuming too many calories with very little nutritious value to it. This will result in you not losing weight. In fact, you might even gain weight.

If you gain weight while fasting, look at your diet. What you eat can change how the fast will affect you. You might have better insulin levels, but you may also have a worse metabolic rate, on top of weight gain. Instead of eating a pint of ice cream every day (you know you want to), try to limit yourself and eat well-balanced meals in between your pints. If you want to lose weight, make sure that your meals are very healthy. This will ensure that the fast impacts you positively.

Myth #6: You'll be Constantly Hungry

This myth is based on fear, pure and simple. We can feel insanely hungry if we just skip a meal. What if we skip 14 hours of meals! In our minds, this sounds terrifying. We think that we'll end up being hungry all the time. Well, we will probably feel some hunger, but it won't be constant. Afterall, if you're not eating for 14 hours, then yes, you're going to feel hungry. But once you eat in your eating window, you will obviously not feel hungry anymore. If you don't believe me, then look at some of the human participants in research, or really an anecdotal evidence from those who have done intermittent fasting.

In some research, when participants completed alternate day fasting, they didn't feel very hungry once they got used to the schedule (Klemple et al., 2010). Of course, this wasn't for all participants, but for many of them, their hunger was reduced. Additionally, you can look at any blog or forum about intermittent fasting, and you'll see that a lot of people talk about how their hunger pangs were reduced after fasting for a bit. Their bodies got used to the fasting schedule, and they felt less hungry during fasting periods or days. Based on this information, it's very unlikely that you'll be constantly hungry.

Chapter 03
Benefits and Risks

After spending so much time tell you what not to believe, we've now come to the chapter that will tell you the great things about intermittent fasting. There are just so many unexpected benefits of fasting, and while I'm sure you started reading this book hoping to just lose weight with fasting, you can gain so many more health benefits than just weight loss. Unfortunately, there's nothing perfect in life, and I'm sad to say that intermittent fasting isn't perfect. There are always some risks and drawbacks of fasting. We'll also cover these in this chapter.

While reading this benefits and risks, keep in mind that not everyone will react the same way. How you react to fasting isn't going to be the same as how someone else does. So, look at your health with a critical eye and consider whether the benefits will help you or whether the risks will harm you. You can also just do a trial and error fast to see how your body will react, but always do so with wisdom.

In this chapter, we'll have some of the research studies mentioned that are about intermittent fasting. It's important to mention some of the limitations of these studies. Intermittent fasting is so recent that there isn't enough research yet on the human experience while intermittent fasting. There is some research, but not a lot. More research has been done on animals that are like humans biologically, like some apes. Some less similar animals are rodents, and there are a lot of studies on fasting with rodents. Some of these will be mentioned here and some will be human studies.

But all will help explain the benefits and risks.

Benefits of Intermittent Fasting

Generally intermittent fasting has way more benefits than risks. The one everyone knows about is weight loss. But there are so many other benefits too. One of the best benefits is how intermittent fasting changes your hormone levels, so that your insulin levels are lowered. There are also some other benefits for your heart, brain, and body.

Weight loss

Weight loss it the most well-known benefit of intermittent fasting. Even this book has the word "weight loss" in the title. During intermittent fasting, it's likely that you'll lose some weight. Whether you're following the easier 14/10 method or the harder alternate day method, you're going to lose some weight. There are a couple of reasons why this is, but the biggest one is because of calorie restriction.

Calorie restriction is one of the most common methods of weight loss recommended by doctors. We've already discussed a bit of how calorie restriction works and how unplanned versus planned calorie restriction works in fasting. In simplified 14/10 fasts and ones like it, you'll have some unplanned calorie restriction which can help you with weight loss. To get the most out of calorie restriction, you would want to follow the alternate day style of fasting. This is because there's just such a massive reduction in calories on those alternate days. Alternate day fasting has been found to be equivalent to regular, doctor approved, calorie reduction in multiple studies (Alhamdan et al., 2016; Klemple et al., 2010; Anson et al., 2003). Even better yet, because calorie reduction is interspersed with full regular meals every other day, this style of fasting is easier to stick with rather than a regular calorie restricted diet. So, you can expect some weight loss while intermittent fasting. However, this also depends on other aspects of your lifestyle. We've talked about the importance of diet before, but we haven't talked about the importance of exercising. Doing regular exercising while intermittent fasting can also increase how much weight you lose, without losing a lot of muscle mass from the fast. You don't have to exercise heavily, but if you want to, you could go for a 30-minute walk, a bike ride or a swim. All of these can help maintain your weight loss while also maintaining your muscle mass.

The last thing to mention is that once you finish your fasting, in the case where you're not doing this for the rest of your life, you'll be less likely to regain the weight. This isn't based on a lot of research, but some people suggest that because fasting changes how you eat and your relationship with food, you don't return to your previous style of eating. Take it or leave it, but you'll still have some improvement in your weight with intermittent fasting.

Intermittent fasting can reduce insulin levels and insulin resistance. Did you know that one-third of Americans are diagnosed with pre-diabetes? That's quite a lot and is often due to our carb and sugar laden diets. So many people in the U.S. struggle with their blood sugar levels and insulin levels. Essentially, in prediabetes your blood sugar levels are consistently higher than normal, and your body tries to fix this by increasing your insulin. Insulin is what helps your body to absorb the glucose from your food to use as energy. However, when experiencing prediabetes, your cells become resistant to the insulin. This increases the cycle again, with more insulin coming into your bloodstream and more insulin resistance occurring. This can be very problematic and result in having a diagnosis of type 2 diabetes, stroke, obesity or heart disease.

Intermittent fasting can help with your insulin levels and insulin resistance.

When intermittent fasting, the blood-glucose levels can be a little more controlled, insulin resistance is reduced, and insulin itself is also reduced. This is something that has been repeated in several studies. The insulin decreases because of the way the body uses the glucose from eating during the fasting period, but it also decreases because of weight loss that is also happening. In most studies, the type of fasting used to create some of the best changes in insulin levels was alternate day fasting. This makes a lot of sense, since it's also the style of fasting that results in the most weight loss.

Improved heart health is one of the benefits that needs to be better researched in humans. However, in animals intermittent fasting is very promising for improving heart health. Intermittent fasting helps improve cholesterol levels, blood pressure, and inflammation. All of which can lead to better heart health. Obviously, this is important because since there are so many things that can negatively affect heart health. So, if intermittent fasting can help reduce these things, then you'll have a lower risk of heart disease, heart attacks, and other cardiovascular problems.

There is some research that suggests intermittent fasting can help with ageing and brain health. It has to do with how your cells recuperate from cellular stress and metabolism. The research suggests that intermittent fasting can help reduce the likelihood of Alzhemiers and Parkinson's diseases (Martin et al., 2009). While this research is very promising, there hasn't been enough human research to say this. However, the promise of better brain health is something to look forward to with intermittent fasting.

Risks of Intermittent Fasting

The risks of intermittent fasting are varied. If people fast when they shouldn't (see chapter 1), then the risks of intermittent fasting can be quite severe. However, for most people intermittent fasting isn't very risky. The risks you'll run into are bingeing, malnutrition, and difficulty with maintaining the fast. We've talked about bingeing quite extensively, so we're not going to discuss it much more. Suffice it to say, bingeing while you fast risks any of the benefits from fasting you might originally have. A bigger risk is malnutrition.

Malnutrition sounds alarming, but for the most part, you can prevent this by having well-balanced meals during your eating windows. The risk of malnutrition comes especially during the kinds of fast which include very low-calorie restriction on fasting days. Fasts like this are 5:2 fasts and alternate day fasting. If you're not eating the right nutrition throughout your week, the reduction in calories plus the poor nutrition can result in some of your dietary needs not being met. This could result in more weight loss, but also more muscle loss and other issues. To prevent this risk, you can ensure that your meals are nutritious and well-balanced. Have a variety of fruits and vegetables, try different meats and seafoods, and include grains unless you're following a specific diet like the keto diet.

Associated with malnutrition is dehydration. We get a lot of our daily water intake from the food we eat. But if you're eating a reduced amount of food during your day, or no food during your day, you're going to need to drink a lot more water than you normally do. If you're not keeping track of your hydration levels, it's possible for you to drink too little. To combat this risk, ensure that you're drinking enough by keeping a hydration journal. You could also track it in an app. Set up reminders to drink water and check your urine color. Light colored urine means good hydration, so check often despite how disgusting it might be to you.

Because fasting can be difficult to start, this can be one of the risks associated with it. You're going to feel hungry during the first couple weeks of following your fasting schedule. You may even feel uncomfortable, with mood swings, different bowel movements, and sleep disruptions. All of this can lead to you struggling with starting the fasts. They can also lead you to ignore greater warning signs that you shouldn't fast. These signs include changed heart rate, feelings of weakness, and extreme fatigue. These feelings shouldn't be ignored during the start. If you feel severely uncomfortable when you start your fast, you should stop and speak with your doctor.

Chapter 04
Styles of Intermittent Fasting

Now that you've learned the basics of intermittent fasting, it's time to go into the different types. There isn't just one style of intermittent fasting. There are basic styles like fasting for a full 24 hours, but there are also other kinds that take advantage of our normal daily activities and leave us slightly less hungry. Whichever method you choose, you'll still receive some good health benefits. There are five different varieties of intermittent fasting that will be covered in this chapter: the 14/10 method, 5:2 method, 24 Hour method, Warrior Diet method, and the Alternate Day method. These five methods have been organized from easiest to hardest. One method that won't be discussed in this chapter is the 16/8 method. It is by far one of the easiest styles of intermittent fasting to get into and to maintain in the longterm. While we won't be covering it in this book, we did write another book that goes into the 16/8 method and provides a step-by-step guide for how to follow it. If you're interested in learning more, please look at Intermittent Fasting 16/8: The Complete Step-by-Step Guide.

14/10 Method

The 14/10 method takes advantage of your daily schedule to add some areas of fasting. It is a type of fasting that is called Time Restricted Eating (TRE). When reading studies about intermittent fasting, you'll see this phrase used often and it is usually referring to the 16/8, 14/10, or 12/12 methods. The 14/10 method is easy to follow, and thus, is a simple way to transition into intermittent fasting. In this method, you fast for 14 hours and then eat during a 10-hour window. It may sound a little difficult, but it isn't. Considering that you'll sleep for some of your 14 hours of fasting, you won't have to fast for as long as you think.

What many people do when they follow this style, is that they extend their fast on both sides of when they go to sleep. For instance, assuming you sleep for eight hours at night, then you'll add three hours of fasting before bed, and three hours after bed. Sometimes this doesn't work for people's schedule, especially if breakfast if important to you. In cases like this, people fast for the extra 6 hours before bed and have their last meal quite early in the day.

Because there isn't a huge shift in how you eat, when you eat, this style of intermittent fasting can be quite beneficial for people. It's something that doesn't change your normal habits very much, which is appealing to many. Afterall, if something new requires a massive change, then you'll be less likely to stick with it. The convenience of the plan also means that you're not going to have a huge difference between when you normally eat and when you eat on the fast. These smaller changes mean that you're more likely to follow the fasting plan and stay motivated to complete it.

Another benefit of this style fast is that you can still make room for social eating, unlike in other plans. If you want to have dinner with your friends, then all you must do is shift your eating and fasting windows so that you can be with your friends. Since this style of fasting doesn't require a different diet, it means that you also won't have to restrict your calories while you're eating out with your friends and family. While a diet isn't a requirement, having a well-balanced meal is recommended.

5:2 Method

This method has recently become more popular. Even comedian Jimmy Kimmel follows this style of fasting, with great results. While the 14/10 method is about when you eat, the 5:2 method is about what and when you eat. This method means that you'll eat regularly for five days a week, but then have two days where you eat a drastically reduced calorie diet. While most people eat roughly 2,200 calories in a day, while you're on the 5:2 fast, you'll eat your 2,200 calories for five days, but then eat only 500-600 calories on the two fasting days.

The benefits of having the calorie restriction twice per week means that you are more likely to lose weight, even if you overeat slightly on the days when you follow your normal diet. The 5:2 diet hasn't been more heavily researched than many other kinds of intermittent fasting, but what has been researched shows some promising studies about it. While many studies are with animals as subjects, there are a few with human participants too.

In some of the studies, it is believed that the 5:2 method can reduce tumors in breast cancer and help with other physiological issues in the body. It can help improve insulin resistance and prevent cardiovascular disease. While these studies are promising, just keep in mind that many of them revolved around animals. You can find the studies in the reference page at the end of this book, if you would like to do further research.

In general, the 5:2 method can provide you with weight loss that is on par with people who reduce calories every day. However, some people find reducing calories every day to be very restrictive. Afterall, there's only so much you can eat on a calorie restrictive diet. However, with the 5:2 method you can eat whatever you want for your eating days, and only reduce your calories on your fasting day. While you can eat whatever you want, you should still maintain a well-balanced diet. Eating only junk food won't help with your weight loss goals, if that is the reason you're choosing to fast.

While the 5:2 method can be very beneficial, some people struggle with their first few fast days. After eating 2,000 calories on day one followed by 500 calories on day two, you can feel almost uncontrollably hungry. However, many people say (anecdotally) that the hunger fades if you keep yourself distracted. Also, so long as you follow the fast for a while, you'll soon no longer feel hungry during your fast days. All of this is anecdotal of course, but it is something to consider when choosing to fast with the 5:2 method.

24 Hour

The 24-hour fast is exactly how it sounds. You simply choose to fast entirely for 24 hours. During this fast, you don't eat at all during your fasting hours, but this doesn't mean that you can't eat during the day of your fast. One-way people cope with the 24 hours of not eating is to start their fast immediately after dinner, and then stop it at the same time the next day. This way, you're still eating on both days, just with a very long time between meals. If this is confusing to you, then here's a clarification: If you finish dinner at 7pm, then that time is your fasting start time. You would continue to fast until 7pm the next day and have your first meal right after that time. This way, you're eating something still, which might help console you.

This timing can be better than if you choose to fast from the moment you wake up one morning to the moment you wake up the next morning. This is how many people first interpret the 24-hour fast, but it is incorrect. If you followed that interpretation, then you would eat dinner at 7pm, maybe have a midnight snack at 12am, fast until you wake up at 8am, and keep fasting until 8am the next day. This places you at 32-37 hours of fasting. So, if you choose to do 24 hours fasting, then really make sure you're counting the 24 hours.

This style of fasting can give you the same benefits as other kinds of intermittent fasting. It provides an overall, weekly calorie reduction, which will lead to weight loss. However, a lot of people can struggle with this kind of fast. Going without food for 24 hours is hard, and can make you feel weak and faint, with low energy levels. On the other hand, some people find it easier to handle than the 5:2 fast, because they think having even a tiny bit of food makes you start craving more. Whichever side of the fence you fall on, the 24-hour fast is still beneficial. Besides feeling a bit hungry during your 24 hours of fasting, there is a likelihood that you'll binge more the next day because you've simply not had anything the day before. Even if you binge a bit, it's unlikely that you'll eat a full day's worth of extra calories. So, you'll still have a weekly calorie reduction.

The Warrior Diet

The Warrior Diet is labelled as a diet, but it's typically a style of intermittent fasting. The Warrior Diet is called such because it's believed to follow the eating habits of ancient warriors. It's based on the belief that warriors would eat very little during the day and then overeat at night in a 'feast.' Essentially, this leads to a 20:4 fast, with 20 hours of fasting, and four hours of eating. Having only four hours to eat can be very difficult for people, especially if you're supposed to overeat. For many of us, having a heavy meal at nighttime can interrupt our sleep habits and can make us feel ill. For others, having to eat so much after a long fast can lead to some gastric distress. So, the Warrior Diet has some areas that people may struggle with.

What you eat is just as important as when you eat during this fast. It's recommended you eat unprocessed foods, with a lot of raw vegetables and fruits. During your 20 hours of fasting, you can eat tiny amounts of fruit and vegetables, but some people will find it difficult to sustain their day on this. With the change in diet and eating time, the Warrior Diet will supposedly cause a clearer mind and better cellular repair. This is possible, since eating less processed food can result in ketosis which helps with cellular repair, and there is some research supporting intermittent fasting for improved brain function. While there isn't a lot of research on the Warrior Diet itself, because it is technically a type of intermittent fasting, some of the research found could carry over to the Warrior Diet. So, it's possible it will lead to weight loss but it's also possible that it won't. There simply isn't enough research out there to promote a 20:4 fast.

The Warrior Diet might work in theory, but it will depend on the type of person who is following it. If you have a lot of dedication, motivation, and a good understanding of nutrition, you could do very well with the Warrior Diet. However, if you're leaving a carbohydrate heavy diet, with three meals a day, the Warrior Diet can be a severe change which can reduce your motivation to continue. Beyond this, with only a four-hour eating window, it can be difficult to do social eating activities, like having brunch, or eating out with your co-workers for lunch. This can strain the motivation and sustainability of those who are trying to follow the diet. This is why it's one of the harder versions of intermittent fasting to follow.

Alternate Day

Alternate Day fasting is like an extended version of the 5:2 method. There's actually a lot of research that supports alternate day fasting, and it's considered to be really good for reducing belly fat in people who are very obese. Even if weight is maintained, there's a good chance that alternate day fasting can lead to better health overall. It can reduce insulin levels and insulin resistance and can help the brain handle cell stress (Anson et al., 2003). There are a lot of studies about it, but as mentioned before, some of these studies are animal studies. However, they provide some promising implications for how alternate day fasting can help humans.

In this fast, you are fasting every other day, and eating your regular portions on your off days. This means that you have an overall reduced calorie load during the week. This is similar to a regular calorie reduction diet, where calories are reduced every day. So, the weekly calorie restriction can be the same in both the fast and the diet. However, people generally find alternate day fasting easier to follow than calorie restricted diets. There are some people who dislike the alternate day fast because it can be very difficult to go hungry during the fasting days. This hunger doesn't always get easier as the weeks go on. This can strain people's motivation to continue the fast. Some people combat this by eating a reduced calorie meal on fasting days. In this case, this adaptation makes the alternate day fast like the 5:2 fast, with just extra days of fasting. Because there is a significant calorie reduction, it's important that the meals you eat are nutritious. You don't want to be undernourished while following this fast. Additionally, if you're already at a healthy weight, this fast may make you lose weight that you can't afford to lose. So be careful when approaching this fast. However, if you are very overweight, then this fast can help you. Just work with your doctor to figure out if this fast will be of benefit to you. As mentioned earlier, there is significant research associated with alternate day fasting, and a lot of it is positive. So, this style of fasting can bring you significant benefits.

To conclude this chapter, there are several different options for following an intermittent fast. You should choose the fasting method that works for you and your lifestyle. If you're a very social eater, then choose a fast like the 14:10 fast or perhaps the 5:2 fast. If you're very determined, have great discipline, and can maintain motivation, then choose a fast like the 24-hour, alternate day, or the Warrior Diet. Either way, you'll likely get some benefits from these fast choices. But with benefits, always comes risks. These fasts all have some risks associated and it's important to know them before choosing to follow intermittent fasting. In the next chapter, we'll be discussing the benefits of fasting in general, and explore the risks associated with fasting.

Chapter 05

Transitioning into Intermittent Fasting

Now we get into the fine print of intermittent fasting. You've learned all the basics of intermittent fasting in general, but it's time to learn how to start your fasts. In this chapter, we'll look at transitioning schedules for each kind of fast. Use the schedules to help you determine which fasts will work for you and which ones are not going to work for your lifestyle. One recommendation I have for you is to track your fast by maintaining a journal. Your journal can help you with your schedule, but also can be a consistent record of which styles have worked for you, which have not, and where you are struggling with the fasts. When you have your journal set up, start by including your chosen fasting schedule and why you've chosen that one. Also add your goals to the journal and write down what works and doesn't for you. Keep it regularly updated and you'll have a beautiful record of your fasting journey.

Before looking at our schedules, there are some things to keep in mind.

• Each of the schedules below will give you some variation of how to startand transition into them. So, when you choose your schedule, you'll have plenty of options to choose from. However, if you don't find a schedule that works for you, then create your own! Each one is personal.

• The schedules don't have to be permanent. Don't feel like you're committed to one type of schedule simply because you've already been using it for several weeks. If it's not working, change it up and choose a different schedule. And if you want to eat out during your fasting window, then just shift your fasting and eating time to fit your social schedule. This isn't an inseparable marriage. Simply choose and adapt your schedule to fit you and don't feel any guilt about changing them as you go along.

• Ideally, you want to transition slowly. So, each schedule will demonstrate a slow transition into the fast. If you don't want to go slow, that's your choice. But going slow will help you ease into the fast and reduce the likelihood of feeling those negative emotions we discussed before. Each of these schedules shows a transition period of two weeks before you're fully following the schedule.

Transitioning into 14:10

When transitioning into the 14:10 schedule, you have a variety of options. You can choose to have an early eating schedule, where your first meal is very early in the morning. You could follow the mid-day eating schedule, or you could follow the late day eating schedule. Choose the one that fits your lifestyle. If you're a shift worker, the late day eating schedule might work best for you. If you're an early morning person, then that schedule will be your best bet. So, choose the one that fits you best.

Early Eating Schedule

If you want to follow your body's natural rhythm of being more active during the early morning, then this is the schedule for you. It's also great because it gives you a decent time in the evening where you'll be without food, which can help you when you sleep. In this schedule, you'll start eating at 7am and end at 5pm. This is a slow transition, so it's a one hour transition every couple of days over the course of two weeks.

TIME	DAY 1-3	DAY 4-6	DAY 7-9	DAY 10-12
7 AM	WAKE UP/EAT	WAKE UP/EAT	WAKE UP/EAT	WAKE UP/EAT
9 AM	EAT	EAT	EAT	EAT
11 AM	EAT	EAT	EAT	EAT
1 PM	EAT	EAT	EAT	EAT
3 PM	EAT	EAT	EAT	EAT
5 PM	EAT	EAT	EAT	EAT BEFORE 5
7 PM	EAT	EAT	FAST	FAST
9 PM	EAT	FAST	FAST	FAST
10 PM	SLEEP/FAST	SLEEP/FAST	SLEEP/FAST	SLEEP/FAST

Once you've transitioned into the fast, here is what your week will look like:

TIME	FROM MONDAY TO SUNDAY
12 AM – 7 AM	SLEEP/FAST
7 AM – 12 PM	BREAKFAST
4 PM – 5 AM	LARGE MEAL (LAST MEAL FINISHED BY 5 AM)
12 AM	SLEEP/FAST

Mid-day Eating Schedule

TIME	DAY 1-3	DAY 4-6	DAY 7-9	DAY 10-12
6 AM	SLEEP/EAT	SLEEP/EAT	SLEEP/EAT	SLEEP/EAT
8 AM	EAT	EAT	FAST	FAST
10 AM	EAT	EAT	EAT	EAT
12 PM	EAT	EAT	EAT	EAT
2 PM	SNACK	SNACK	EAT	EAT
4 PM	EAT	EAT	EAT	EAT
6 PM	EAT	EAT	EAT	EAT
9 PM	EAT	EAT	EAT	EAT BEFORE 8
10 PM	SLEEP/FAST	SLEEP/FAST	SLEEP/FAST	SLEEP/FAST

The mid-day eating schedule works for people who aren't morning people. It's also something that you can follow on the weekends, if you want a later start to your day. This schedule is also great because you can have more of a social life than in the early eating schedule. After all, most people eat dinner out socially usually after 5pm. Again, this schedule is a transition over the course of a couple of weeks. This may help reduce your feelings of discomfort as you transition. In this schedule, you start eating at 10am and finish your last meal by 8pm.

Once you've transitioned into the fast, here is what your week will look like:

TIME	FROM MONDAY TO SUNDAY
12 AM – 7 AM	SLEEP/FAST
10 AM – 2 PM	BREAKFAST
7 PM – 8 PM	LARGE MEAL (LAST MEAL FINISHED BY 8 PM)
12 PM	SLEEP/FAST

Evening Eating Schedule

Many people have difficulty eating late at night. However, if you're a night owl and want to have later meals, this schedule is for you. There are some things to notice about this schedule. First is that our bodies don't normally metabolize food efficiently at night. So, you may have difficulty sleeping if you eat too late, and you won't have the same benefits with glucose as you would by eating early in the day. However, this schedule is perfect if you plan on partying with your friends late at night, or if you work unconventional hours. Just like before, this fast transitions over the course of a couple weeks.

Your eating window starts at 2pm and ends at 12am.

TIME	DAY 1-3	DAY 4-6	DAY 7-9	DAY 10-12
12 AM-6AM	SLEEP/FAST	SLEEP/FAST	SLEEP/FAST	SLEEP/FAST
8 AM	EAT	FAST	FAST	FAST
10 AM	EAT	EAT	FAST	FAST
12 PM	EAT	EAT	EAT	FAST
2 PM	SNACK	EAT	EAT	EAT
4 PM	EAT	EAT	SNACK	EAT
6 PM	EAT	SNACK	EAT	EAT
8 PM	EAT	EAT	EAT	EAT
10 PM	EAT	EAT	EAT	EAT
12 AM	EAT	EAT	EAT	EAT BEFORE MIDNIGHT

Once you've transitioned into the fast, here is what your week will look like:

TIME	FROM MONDAY TO SUNDAY
12 AM – 8 AM	SLEEP/FAST
8 AM – 2 PM	FAST
7 PM – 11 PM	BREAKFAST
12 PM	LARGE MEAL (LAST MEAL FINISHED BEFORE MIDNIGHT)

With these three schedules, you have a variety of opportunities to fast following the 14/10 method. Make sure that you take the time to make these schedules yours. Adapt them to your schedule and your family situation. You can also shift your schedule over a couple of days. If the early morning schedule appeals to you, but you like having dinner out with friends every Friday night, then you may choose to shift your eating windows for the weekend. This way you're still fasting for 14 hours and eating within a 10hour window.

Transitioning into 5:2

The 5:2 schedule is different from the 14/10 schedule. It doesn't require a daily fast, but instead requires two days of fasting within the week. During those two days, you'll eat just 500-600 calories for that day. In this section, we'll look at two possible schedules for your 5:2 fast. The first schedule is one where you fast on Mondays and Thursdays. The second option is a fast on Wednesdays and Saturdays. If you choose to create your own schedule, make sure that you have a couple of days between each fasting day. Don't fast for Saturday and Sunday. That's 48 hours with limited calories and isn't good for your body. You'll also feel incredibly hungry by the time you eat on Monday. So, if you are following your own schedule, make sure you have a couple of days between each fasting day.

Monday and Thursday fasting days

This schedule is perfect for those who are comfortable being at work without much food. For some of us, this doesn't work. However, if you feel very comfortable with it, then this schedule will work for you. Remember that during your fasting days, you can eat 500-600 calories. During your eating days, you can eat what you want, but try not to overeat or you'll undo the good you did during your fast. This schedule will transition you over the course of a couple of weeks.

Week 1:

TIME	MON	TUE	WED	THURS	FRI	SAT	SUN
8 AM	FAST	EAT ALL DAY	EAT ALL DAY	FAST	EAT ALL DAY	EAT ALL DAY	EAT ALL DAY
12 PM	EAT 800 CAL	EAT	EAT	EAT 600 CAL	EAT	EAT	EAT
4 PM	EAT	EAT	EAT	EAT	EAT	EAT	EAT
8 PM	EAT 400 CAL	EAT	EAT	EAT 400 CAL	EAT	EAT	EAT
10 PM	SLEEP/ FAST	SLEEP/ FAST	SLEEP/ FAST	SLEEP/ FAST	EAT	EAT	EAT
12 AM	SLEEP/ FAST	SLEEP/ FAST	SLEEP/ FAST	SLEEP/ FAST	SLEEP/ FAST	SLEEP/ FAST	SLEEP/ FAST

TIME	MON	TUE	WED	THURS	FRI	SAT	SUN
8 AM	FAST	EAT ALL DAY	EAT ALL DAY	FAST	EAT ALL DAY	EAT ALL DAY	EAT ALL DAY
12 PM	EAT 400 CAL	EAT	EAT	EAT 400 CAL	EAT	EAT	EAT
4 PM	FAST	EAT	EAT	FAST	EAT	EAT	EAT
8 PM	EAT 300 CAL	EAT	EAT	EAT 300 CAL	EAT	EAT	EAT
10 PM	SLEEP/ FAST	SLEEP/ FAST	SLEEP/ FAST	SLEEP/ FAST	EAT	EAT	EAT
12 AM	SLEEP/ FAST	SLEEP/ FAST	SLEEP/ FAST	SLEEP/ FAST	SLEEP/ FAST	SLEEP/ FAST	SLEEP/ FAST

Week 2:

You can see in this schedule; you're increasing your fasting time from week one to week two on your fasting days. There's also a mid-day fast within week two. When you fully transition into your fast, your week will look like this:

MON	Fast day: Eat 500-600 calories through the day, or eat one large meal
TUE	Eating day: Eat what you want, but don't overeat. Break your fast carefully
WED	Eating day
THURS	Fast day: Eat 500-600 calories through the day, or eat one large meal
FRI	Eating day: Eat what you want, but don't overeat. Break your fast carefully
SAT	Eating day
SUN	Eating day

In the schedule above, you should have noticed the additional note to break your fast carefully. Because you'll be breaking your fast after a day with very low calories, you want to break it slowly. Start your breakfast with something that is light, not too heavy, and not something sugary. If you don't, you may feel some gastric upset and nausea. So, break your fast with some tea or bone broth, have a bit of yogurt and nuts, or something else light for you. Once you break your fast, you can eat normally throughout the day. There's more about breaking your fast in the section on transitioning into the 24 hours fast.

Wednesday and Saturday fasting days

This schedule works well for those who want to fast over a weekend day. This can be great if you tend to feel faint or very hungry when fasting. It can also be less distracting than if you're sitting at work watching everyone eat donuts and coffee while you're fasting. This schedule might not work for you if you're a very social eater over the weekends. So, take that into consideration before choosing this schedule.

TIME	MON	TUE	WED	THURS	FRI	SAT	SUN
8 AM	EAT ALL DAY	EAT ALL DAY	FAST	EAT ALL DAY	EAT ALL DAY	FAST	EAT ALL DAY
12 PM	EAT	EAT	EAT 800 CAL	EAT	EAT	EAT 600 CAL	EAT
4 PM	FAST	EAT	EAT	FAST	EAT	EAT	EAT
8 PM	EAT	EAT	EAT 400 CAL	EAT	EAT 400 CAL	EAT	EAT
10 PM	SLEEP/ FAST	SLEEP/ FAST	SLEEP/ FAST	SLEEP/ FAST	EAT	EAT	EAT
12 AM	SLEEP/ FAST	SLEEP/ FAST	SLEEP/ FAST	SLEEP/ FAST	SLEEP/ FAST	SLEEP/ FAST	SLEEP/ FAST

Week 1

TIME	MON	TUE	WED	THURS	FRI	SAT	SUN
8 AM	EAT ALL DAY	EAT ALL DAY	FAST	EAT ALL DAY	EAT ALL DAY	FAST	EAT ALL DAY
12 PM	EAT	EAT	EAT 400 CAL	EAT	EAT	EAT 400 CAL	EAT
4 PM	FAST	EAT	EAT	FAST	EAT	EAT	EAT
8 PM	EAT	EAT	EAT 400 CAL	EAT	EAT 300 CAL	EAT	EAT
10 PM	SLEEP/ FAST	SLEEP/ FAST	SLEEP/ FAST	SLEEP/ FAST	EAT	FAST	EAT
12 AM	SLEEP/ FAST	SLEEP/ FAST	SLEEP/ FAST	SLEEP/ FAST	SLEEP/ FAST	SLEEP/ FAST	SLEEP/ FAST

Week 2

When you fully transition into your fast, your week will look like this:

MON	Eating all day
TUE	Eating all day
WED	Fast day: Eat 500-600 calories through the day, or eat one large meal
THURS	Eating day: Eat what you want, but don't overeat. Break your fast carefully
FRI	Eating day
SAT	Fast day: Eat 500-600 calories through the day, or eat one large meal
SUN	Eating day: Eat what you want, but don't overeat. Break your fast carefully

In both these fasting plans, you'll notice that there are some recommendations for how many calories to eat on your fasting days as you transition. These are recommendations, with the hope that it will be easier to do the full fast in week three. However, shifting to such few calories can be a little jarring. So, if you need to take it slower, go ahead! Do whatever help your body adjust to the fast best. These plans put 'breakfast' as the largest meal and it's the one that shifts to fewer and fewer calories for the fasting days. This is because it's better to have a larger meal in the morning than in the evening.

For your fasting days, you can choose to eat your 500-600 calories all in one meal, or you may choose to break it up over a couple meals/snacks. In these plans we put them as two meals, but it can also be an all-day grazing situation. You could just snack on fruits and vegetables throughout the day, with some protein interspersed. This can help you feel fuller throughout your day, rather than just eating one large meal. However, you want to choose what you'll do based on your situation. We'll discuss some options for meals in a later chapter.

Transitioning into 24 Hour Fast

This fast is very flexible, as there's no requirement for which day you choose to fast. The only thing to keep in mind is that you don't want to fast two days in a row. Keep it at just 24 hours, and no longer.

This is to ensure that you're not starting your body's starvation response with further fasting.

For this fast style, there is only one example schedule. This is just to give you an idea of how to time your 24 hours, so you still have a meal every day, while still having a 24-hour window where you're not eating. In this schedule, the fasting days are on Saturday and Tuesday. Because there isn't a set day requirement for this fast, you could choose just to fast one day, or two days in the week. If you want to fast three days, that's moving into the alternate day fasting, which we'll talk about later in this chapter.

Here is your schedule into 24 hours fasting. There isn't a transitioning period for this one, since when you choose to fast is completely random.

For this kind of fast, choose to fast on the days when you won't need to do a lot of physical work. If your job if physically demanding, then fast on weekends or days when you won't work. If you just like working out a lot, then on your fasting days, you'll want to take it easy or skip all together. Whatever you do, if you decide to exercise while on this fast, make sure it's right before you break your fast. You want to eat a good mix of protein and fiber after exercising to help your muscles recover.

With a 24 hour fast, it's very important that you maintain your hydration levels. Have water, tea, and black coffee during your fast. This will help with your hunger, but also help you stay hydrated. Becoming dehydrated will cause you some damage, especially because you're not getting your hydration from food. So, keep drinking liquids throughout your day, and regularly check your hydration.

In this fast and in other 24-hour style fasts, you will want to be careful with how you break your fast.

What to Eat to Break your Fast

Once you've survived your 24 hours fast, it's time to eat again. You're going to feel hungry. There's no way around it but you might feel intensely hungry. The last thing you want to do is gorge yourself on all the food. It's possible it will all just right back up if you do so, and you'll also lose some of the benefits you received from the fast in the first place. To prevent difficulty with eating again, it's important to take things slow as you break your fast.

Start by eating a little snack such as some blueberries. Starting with a liquid like water, tea, or coffee can be a great option. Another option is to have bone broth. This will help you feel fuller, but also provide you with some good nutrients for starting your eating window. After having some liquids and a small snack, 10 minutes later eat something a bit more substantial.

You're going to want to change your food type for breaking your fast. While a bacon burger will be so tempting, it's not the best choice to break your fast. It's way too heavy, too fatty, and too much for your first meal. It can make you feel bloated, have indigestion, or make you sick to your stomach. So, if you're desperate for that burger, eat it later, long after you've broken your fast. Instead of a burger, have some light proteins and fibers. Choose some fruit that aren't going to spike your blood-sugar, like raspberries, and eat them with some yogurt.

Add some sunflower or flax seeds to your yogurt for added nutrition.

Some people have a lot of difficulty with eating something sugary or full of carbs after a fast. It can cause you to feel bloated and miserable. It spikes your blood sugar very quickly after a period of having lower blood-sugar levels because of your fast. This can be jarring and result in some negative physical responses. However, some people are really used to eating sweetened cereal for breakfast or even Pop Tarts. If you are desperate for your oatmeal in the morning after a fast, then go ahead and eat some. Check how your body feels while and after eating. This can give you a good idea for how you respond to eating these foods after a long fast. If you find that you feel miserable, then you know to avoid those foods when breaking your fast. If you feel fine, then go ahead and stick with your normal routine.

Transitioning into the Warrior Diet

This section is more about a 20:4 intermittent fast, rather than the warrior diet itself. The warrior diet has its own transitioning recommendations, which may or may not work for everyone. It can be intense, requiring significant diet changes while also changing when you eat — all of which take place at the same time and right at the beginning of the diet. So, this can be difficult to start. For this reason, this section will talk about how to transition into a 20:4 fasting schedule over the course of a couple weeks.

Like we did for the 14:10 fast, we'll provide you with some different fasting schedules that might fit your lifestyle. Once you've transitioned, you'll have a 20hour fasting window.

Early eating schedule

This schedule is perfect if you don't want to skip breakfast. In fact, there are a lot of people that say you shouldn't skip breakfast at all. This is partially because of your circadian rhythm. Your body is more primed to activity in the morning than in the evening. So, eating your meals in the morning can have the most benefit to you. By following the early morning schedule, you won't be going to bed on a full stomach. Sleeping with so much digestion happening can be nightmare inducing. Literally. But it can also cause you to have a restless sleep, have less energy in the morning, and just in general feel terrible. So, the early morning eating schedule is perfect for those who want to avoid these difficulties.

This fasting schedule opens the eating window at 7am and ends the eating window at 11am

TIME	DAY 1-3	DAY 4-6	DAY 7-9	DAY 10-12
7 AM	WAKE UP EAT	WAKE UP EAT	WAKE UP EAT	WAKE UP EAT
9 AM	EAT	EAT	EAT	EAT
11 AM	EAT	EAT	EAT	EAT BEFORE 11
1 PM	EAT	EAT	EAT	FAST
3 PM	EAT	EAT	FAST	FAST
5 PM	EAT	EAT	FAST	FAST
7 PM	EAT	FAST	FAST	FAST
9 PM	FAST	FAST	FAST	FAST
10 PM	SLEEP/FAST	SLEEP/FAST	SLEEP/FAST	SLEEP/FAST

Here is your schedule for the 20 hours fast:

As you can see in this schedule, it's a very significant change every three days. This should help you shift into your 20 hours of fasting, but if you're finding it difficult, then go slower before going into the 20 hours.

Once you've transitioned into the fast, you'll have a weekly schedule that looks like this:

TIME	FROM MONDAY TO SUNDAY
12 AM – 8 AM	SLEEP/FAST
8 AM – 2 PM	BREAKFAST (LAST MEAL FINISHED BY 11 AM)
2 PM – 7 PM	FAST
11 PM - 12 AM	SLEEP/FAST

This schedule can put a strain on your social eating. If you want to eat out with friends, you can adjust your eating window, but don't do a drastic adjustment. If you abruptly change your eating window, then it's possible that you'll have more than 24 hours of fasting and this can be very jarring if you're not prepared for it.

Mid-day eating schedule

This fasting window is perfect for those who are comfortable with eating a lot during work. It's also a good window if you want to have social lunches to eat with your friends and family. Because this window is still early in the day, you'll avoid the difficulties with late night eating mentioned in the first schedule. This fasting schedule opens your eating window at 11am and closes it at 3pm.

TIME	DAY 1-3	DAY 4-6	DAY 7-9	DAY 10-12
6 AM	SLEEP/FAST	SLEEP/FAST	SLEEP/FAST	SLEEP/FAST
9 AM	EAT	EAT	FAST	FAST
11 AM	EAT	EAT	EAT	EAT
1 PM	EAT	EAT	EAT	EAT
3 PM	EAT	EAT	EAT	EAT BEFORE 3
5 PM	EAT	EAT	EAT	FAST
7 PM	EAT	EAT	FAST	FAST
9 PM	EAT	FAST	FAST	FAST
10 PM	SLEEP/FAST	SLEEP/FAST	SLEEP/FAST	SLEEP/FAST

Here is your fasting schedule for the midday eating window:

Once you've transitioned into your fast, you'll have a weekly schedule that looks like this:

TIME	FROM MONDAY TO SUNDAY
12 AM – 8 AM	SLEEP/FAST
8 AM – 2 PM	FAST
2 PM – 7 PM	BREAKFAST (LAST MEAL FINISHED BY 3 PM)
11 PM - 12 AM	SLEEP/FAST

Evening eating schedule

This schedule is perfect if you do a lot of social eating and want to be able to eat with your friends and family at nighttime. The downside to this schedule is that it ends late enough that you may experience some discomfort while you sleep. Many people have nightmares if they eat before bed, especially if they eat a lot. You may also have a very restless sleep. If you stay up all night, then this fast will work for you.

In this schedule, your eating window opens at 6pm and closes at 10pm

TIME	DAY 1-3	DAY 4-6	DAY 7-9	DAY 10-12
6 AM	SLEEP/FAST	SLEEP/FAST	SLEEP/FAST	SLEEP/FAST
8 AM	FAST	FAST	FAST	FAST
10 AM	EAT	FAST	FAST	FAST
12 PM	EAT	EAT	FAST	FAST
2 PM	SNACK	EAT	EAT	FAST
4 PM	EAT	EAT	EAT	FAST
6 PM	EAT	EAT	EAT	EAT
9 PM	EAT	EAT	EAT	EAT BEFORE 10
11 PM	SLEEP/FAST	SLEEP/FAST	SLEEP/FAST	SLEEP/FAST

Here is your fasting schedule for late evening meals:

Once you've transitioned into your fast, you'll have a weekly schedule that looks like this:

TIME	FROM MONDAY TO SUNDAY
12 AM – 8 AM	SLEEP/FAST
8 AM – 2 PM	FAST
2 PM – 7 PM	FAST
11 PM - 12 AM	BREAKFAST (LAST MEAL FINISHED BY 10 PM)

While the warrior diet is a kind of intermittent fasting, it's very difficult to follow and not recommended for most people. You'll need to eat a lot during those four hours to maintain your nutrition, and this can be quite difficult. Eating 2,000 calories within four hours is nearly impossible, so you'll have significant calorie reductions during your day. You need to ensure you eat at minimum, 1300 calories during your eating windows to help you stay healthy. Each of your meals also must be nutritious and well-balanced. If you only eat food without a lot of nutrients, but with a lot of calories, you'll end up not having enough nutrients in your diet.

During your fasting window, the official warrior diet recommends you have liquids like broth, juice, water, and vegetable juice. They also recommend eating some dairy during the fasting window. Dairy like hard boiled eggs is allowed during the fasting period. This might make it a bit easier to follow the rest of the schedule. It will also help ease your hunger.

If you want to try this type of fast, take your time and pay close attention to your body. Check-in with yourself regularly. If you find that people are becoming increasingly annoying and irritating to you, and that the hunger never ends, then this fast is not for you. Ease back into a simpler 14:10 fast or 16:8 fast.

Transitioning into Alternate Day Fasting

Alternate day fasting is the kind of fast that has the most research associated and can lead to the most gains with fasting. So, it's easy to see how it can be a very popular choice. Even though it's beneficial, it's also hard to follow. It is a 24-hour style of fast, but it happens every other day instead of just once or twice a week. The transition into this will be like the 24 hours fast. There isn't going to be a huge transition period. You just must dive in. You'll have a meal every day, but during your fasting window, you won't have any meals. This is the traditional way to do alternate day fasting. If this is too difficult for you, you could add 500 calories to your fasting days, like you would for the 5:2 fasting method. Here is one possible fasting schedule with alternate day fasting:

TIME	MON	TUE	WED	THURS	FRI	SAT	SUN	MON
6 AM	SLEEP/ FAST	SLEEP/ FAST	SLEEP/ FAST	SLEEP/ FAST	SLEEP/ FAST	SLEEP/ FAST	SLEEP/ FAST	SLEEP/ FAST
8 AM	EAT	FAST	EAT ALL DAY	EAT	FAST	EAT ALL DAY	EAT	FAST
10 AM	EAT	FAST	EAT	EAT	FAST	EAT	EAT	FAST
12 PM	EAT	FAST	EAT	EAT	FAST	EAT	EAT	FAST
2 PM	EAT	FAST	EAT	EAT	FAST	EAT	EAT	FAST
4 PM	EAT	FAST	EAT	EAT	FAST	EAT	EAT	FAST
6 PM	FINISH EATING BY 8PM	FAST	EAT	FINISH EATING BY 8PM	FAST	EAT	FINISH EATING BY 8PM	FAST
8 PM	FAST	BREAKFAST	FAST	FAST	BREAKFAST	EAT	FAST	BREAKFAST
10 PM	FAST	EAT	FAST	FAST	EAT	EAT	FAST	EAT

In this schedule, you have some days without any fasting at all, but each day also has an eating window. This can be helpful if you struggle with having no food at all during the day. You can see how the next week starts on the opposite schedule. The whole point is to alternate days for eating and fasting, so each week will be a little different.

If you want to follow a schedule that looks more like an alternate day one, then you can follow this schedule:

TIME	MON	TUE	WED	THURS	FRI	SAT	SUN	MON
6 AM	SLEEP/ FAST	SLEEP/ FAST	SLEEP/ FAST	SLEEP/ FAST	SLEEP/ FAST	SLEEP/ FAST	SLEEP/ FAST	SLEEP/ FAST
8 AM	EAT	FAST	EAT	FAST	EAT	FAST	EAT	FAST
10 AM	EAT	FAST	EAT	FAST	EAT	FAST	EAT	FAST
12 PM	EAT	FAST	EAT	FAST	EAT	FAST	EAT	FAST
2 PM	EAT	FAST	EAT	FAST	EAT	FAST	EAT	FAST
4 PM	EAT	FAST	EAT	FAST	EAT	FAST	EAT	FAST
6 PM	EAT	FAST	EAT	FAST	EAT	FAST	EAT	FAST
8 PM	EAT	FAST	EAT	FAST	EAT	FAST	EAT	FAST
10 PM	EAT	FAST	EAT	FAST	EAT	FAST	EAT	FAST

This schedule is not recommended unless you're really determined. You'll see that you are already fasting while you're asleep and continue your fast into the day until the next morning. This can put you close to a 32 hour fast, so it's recommended that you follow the first alternate day schedule, and not the second. However, if you're determined to follow this kind of schedule, then choose to eat 500-600 calories on your fasting days. This can help you deal with the hunger during your fast.

Hopefully, with all these scheduling options, you'll be able to find a type of intermittent fasting that works for you. If you haven't, that's okay! Just adjust one of these schedules to better fit your life. Try not to fast beyond 24 hours at a time, but if you choose to extend your fast, then ensure you eat a small meal to help carry you over your fast. In the next chapter, we will explore some possible meal plans for intermittent fasting.

Chapter 06
Intermittent Fasting and Your Diet

We've talked a lot about the why, how, and when of intermittent fasting. Let's now look at your diet and how it can help you with fasting. There are some diets that are specific to intermittent fasts. For example, the 5:2 method and alternate day fasting both have the option of having small, calorie restricted meals during your fasting days. Most other fasts simply require you to have no food during the fasting window, and during the eating window, eating well balanced meals. The Warrior Diet recommends following a Paleo style diet to bet the most benefits from it. We'll cover all these diet options for fasting. Just remember to eat what works for you. If you don't want to change your diet, you don't have to. Afterall, intermittent fasting isn't a diet, so you don't have to change if you don't want to. However, if you don't currently have a good diet, a change to a healthier one will help you, with or without intermittent fasting. So, we'll cover some well-balanced meals and nutrition for regular eating without restriction.

5:2 Method and Alternate Day: Calorie Restriction

In the 5:2 method and some alternate day methods, you can eat a restricted diet of 500-600 calories during your fasting window. This helps to curb hunger, and reduce your calorie intake over the course of a week. Your reduction in calories can help with putting your body in ketosis to burn more fat and can also result in more weight loss in comparison to fasting alone.

With these two methods, you're getting the best of both worlds and some of the best health benefits of intermittent fasting.

A reduction from 2,000 calories a day to 600 calories can feel quite drastic. So long as you are eating your regular amount of food during your eating days, you'll be okay nutrition and health wise. To get the most out of the calorie reduction, eat a combination of protein and fiber. These two food kinds can help reduce your hunger and keep you fuller, longer. Depending on how you want to eat throughout your day, your meals are going to vary. Some people divide their allotted calories between two meals. Some people eat one large meal with all the calories for their day in it. Some people simply snack on a variety of low-calorie foods throughout the day. Let's explore some meal types that you could have with calorie restriction. The meals mentioned here will also mention their calories so you can determine how much to eat. You can also use websites and apps to give you more recipe suggestions. Whatever you choose to eat, you need to take the time to either follow the recipe precisely or weigh out your food. This way, you'll have a precise measurement of how many calories you're eating. If you choose to snack throughout the day, we'll provide some snacking options.

It's critically important that you eat at least 1,800 calories on your eating days. This is to ensure that you have enough nutrition to last both your eating day, and your fasting days. You don't want to put too much stress on your body and make it think that you're starving yourself. If you're worried about your diet, talk to a nutritionist to ensure you're eating enough, and getting good nutrients from your meals.

During your fasting window, you could eat 600 calories of marshmallows, but they're not going to provide you with the nutrients you need. So, the ideas mentioned here for your diet contain a good mix of light proteins, fruits, vegetables, and low-fat dairy. There are also a lot of egg recipes, because eggs are amazing, and healthy.

Breakfast ideas

There are a lot of foods out there that are going to provide you with a filling meal, with little calories. These include vegetables and eggs. For breakfast, you want to mix some protein with fiber, and this works perfectly with vegetables and eggs, or fruit and yogurt. The meals in this section are all 300 calories or less. You can follow these ideas to help you choose good breakfast options. If they're not filling enough, add vegetables or fruit that are low in calories. Here are our breakfast recommendations, all for under 300 calories:

- An English muffin with cream cheese and spinach. Add some salt and red pepper to spice it up. Follow the regular serving size of cream cheese to keep the calories low.

- One apple, sliced up, and peanut butter. An apple is about 120 calories, so adjust the peanut butter amount to make up 300 calories.

- Vegetables, egg, and feta cheese frittata. Choose a low-fat variety of cheese to reduce calories. Many vegetables like zucchini are low in calories, so you could probably use a quarter zucchini and one egg per serving in the frittata.

- One cup of whole-grain cereal, with one cup of milk and fruit on the side. Choosing a whole grain cereal will help get you some good fiber. The milk is your protein.

- Oatmeal with fruit is another tasty and wholesome option. If you want to add some sugar to it, then adjust the other calories in the meal. You can also make your oatmeal with water or milk. Just adjust to accommodate your calorie intake accordingly.

- Two scrambled eggs with one piece of whole grain toast. Add some butter to your toast but check your portion size to keep the calories low. Margarine isn't recommended because it's not a healthy fat and doesn't provide you any health benefits.

- One slice of whole grain bread with peanut butter and topped with sliced bananas.

-

While you eat these meals, or any other meals you choose, make sure that you keep a record of how your body reacts to these meals. Do they help alleviate your hunger during a longer fast? Do they make you feel uncomfortable? Just be mindful of what you eat and how it makes you feel while eating these very low-calorie meals.

Lunch and dinner ideas

These two meal times are combined for this section simply because many of the meals are good for lunch or dinner. Pretty straightforward. These meals also try to combine protein and fiber so that you won't be too hungry. Eat of these meals are about 300 calories, and a lot of them are soup and salad!

Soup is a great way to get your nutrients in an easily portioned meal. Salad is also fantastic because you can add a lot of leafy greens which are all very low-calorie vegetables. They keep you feeling full, but also provide you with essential nutrients.

• A jacket potato with salsa, sour cream, and perhaps a smidge of cheese. Cheese is delicious, so don't overdo it. Add some chives to give a bit more flavor.

• Fresh rolls with shrimp and a lot of vegetables. Vegetables that work in fresh rolls are spinach, sliced red peppers, sliced cucumbers or radishes. Use them individually or all together for some excellent flavor. Add some sauce on the side, like soy sauce or peanut sauce to dip your fresh rolls in. Avoid sauces full of sugar.

• Onion and potato pancakes with a side salad. This meal doesn't provide a lot of protein, so you can add a boiled egg to your side salad to help with that. But that's more calories.

• One baked chicken thigh with potatoes and swiss chard. Swiss chard can be bitter, so if this isn't a flavor profile you like, substitute with another cooked, leafy green. This meal is really filling and an excellent combination of protein and fiber.

• Winter squash and silken tofu soup. It sounds strange, but silken tofu is perfect for soups and smoothies. In this recipe, cook the squash first with your flavorings and broth, then blend it with tofu. You'll have a perfect protein and fiber combination.

- Pork ragù and polenta. This meal is very comforting and yet can provide you with good protein and fiber, plus a lot of flavor. Just check your portion sizes to ensure you're eating the right amount.

- Chicken and orzo soup. Add a lot of vegetables to the soup to provide you with more fiber.

- Cheese and broccoli soup. This doesn't sound low calorie, but it can be if you reduce how much fat you put into it. Use chicken or vegetable broth, skim or 1% milk, and only a few ounces of cheese.

This will help keep the calories down and will also provide you with a delicious, warming soup.

Salads are also a great option for lunch or dinner. The key here is to have a lot of leafy greens and watch your extras. It's very easy to go overboard with a salad. Sometimes dressings can also be full of calories. You could make your own dressing by combining an oil with an acidic ingredient. For example, olive oil and lemon juice make a beautiful dressing. So does red wine vinegar and olive oil. Choose your dressing wisely and keep your toppings down. Adding protein and other toppings can provide you with a fuller meal, while also satisfying your taste buds. Some protein choices you can add to salad include shredded chicken, shrimp, tuna, beans, hard-boiled eggs or cooked tofu. All of this can satisfy the protein plus fiber combination which will tide you over your fast. Other toppings could be avocado, cheese, nuts, or seeds. While these are all delicious, you'll need to keep your portion sizes in check since it can easily exceed your calorie requirements. Nuts for example are very calorie dense. So, go easy with these kinds of toppings. Here are some salad ideas for your fast:

- Scallops and watercress. Watercress is a good option if you're bored with lettuce or spinach. You could also add crumbled bacon onto your salad for more flavor if you want to.

- Steak and arugula salad. Again, arugula is a good alternative to regular leafy greens in a salad.

Arugula is perfect and slightly spicy, giving you a lot of flavor. For more flavor, add some shaved parmesan.

• Grilled corn and pepper salad with shrimp. This salad has no leafy greens, but you can add some to get a more filling lunch or dinner.

• Chickpea, cucumber, and tomato salad. Add some red onion for additional flavor if you want to. If the protein isn't enough for you, replace it with some shredded chicken.

• Caprese salad. This salad is basically mozzarella cheese and sliced tomatoes. Check how much mozzarella you use to make sure you don't go overboard.

Snacking ideas

Having one or two large meals in your day may not be your chosen style. In this case, you should consider snacking over the course of the day to stave off hunger. Your snacks could be large, or simply things to munch on. So long as you're not exceeding 600 calories on your fasting day, you should be okay. Make sure you that you keep a record of how many calories you're eating in your day, by tracking on an app or journal. Here are some snacking ideas for your reduced calorie days.

• Turkey slices and cheese slices. Try to keep it to two slices of deli turkey and two slices of deli cheese. Add some crackers or half a pita.

Some sliced cucumbers and carrots can also go beautifully with it.

• Various colored grape tomatoes, two hard boiled eggs, and some wheat crackers. The number of crackers and type of crackers you choose depends on how many calories each is. Make sure you check carefully and eat the right amount.

• Sliced cucumbers and radishes. You can dip them in a little plain yogurt or hummus for some protein.

• Roasted carrots. They're delicious, so nothing else is really needed unless you want to add more flavor.

• A handful of nuts. Since nuts are calorie dense, keep their number low.

•   Half a cup of frozen yogurt. The perfect dessert that also provides some protein.

•   A package of plain popcorn. Popcorn is high in fiber and very filling. You won't need to eat a lot and 100 calories worth of popcorn will fill you up. If you want to add flavors, adjust your calorie count accordingly.

•   A medley of fruits. This is just a fancy name for some sliced up fruits to munch on. Some good options are clementine segments, sliced apples, strawberries, and sliced kiwi. They're delicious together or on their own.

•   A cup of watermelon. Watermelon is a great snack. It provides so much hydration, but also some key vitamins and electrolytes.

•   A grapefruit cut in half. This is a perfect tart dessert. If you want to, sprinkle a little sugar on it for added sweetness.

•   Low fat yogurt cup and a handful of blueberries. Yogurt can be really filling and satisfying when you're hungry. Try to avoid ones that have fruit on the bottom since they have a lot of sugar in them. Instead, get a reduced sugar variety, or even eat it plain.

•   Vegetable plates. You often find these when you go to a party. Having a plate of carrots, broccoli, sliced bell peppers, and celery can be an excellent snacking option. They'll keep you full but with very few calories.

•   String cheese. If cheese is what you crave the most, this can help satisfyyou. String cheese isn't a lot of calories and is an excellent source of dairy and protein.

When you choose to snack, you still need to count your calories. Don't gorge until you're full just because all of these are low calorie snacks. A lot of low-calorie items add up to significant calorie gains very quickly. This can derail your goals for weekly calorie reduction. So, make sure you measure how much you eat and keep a record of it.

Warrior Diet: Paleo

The food for the warrior diet is different than the food requirements for the 5:2 method and the alternate day method. The warrior diet doesn't require any calorie reduction at all. In also doesn't really have restricted foods. However, a lot of people recommend following the paleo diet while also doing the warrior diet. Since the paleo diet is healthy, this recommendation isn't really going to harm you.

Just remember to eat enough nutrients during your four-hour window to remain healthy.

The paleo diet is one based on our ancestors' lives. It recommends eating foods that were similarly available in antiquity. So, there is a heavy emphasis on protein like seafood, eggs, and meat. It also emphasizes fruits and vegetables, nuts and seeds, and healthy fats. The paleo diet doesn't allow most grains, sugars, legumes or dairy. Afterall, these were based on heavy agriculture and processing. In general, unprocessed food is recommended over processed foods. So, if it's anything that has been processed, it should be avoided while on the paleo diet.

Since there isn't a calorie restriction when following the warrior diet, the calories will not be included, or really considered, in the foods mentioned in this section. These food options are paleo and will provide you with good nutrition. Just ensure you are getting enough variety to maintain your nutrition. So, don't eat way more protein than any other food group. Mix it up. While grains are prohibited in paleo diets, you can adapt it to fit your lifestyle better. Some people who follow paleo eat rice as their grain.

Breakfast ideas

Depending on your fasting schedule, you may not have a typical breakfast. Afterall, you might just break your fast at 6pm instead of 6am However, the meals can be the same or similar. Remember, before eating this breakfast meal, have something small a couple minutes before, just to readjust your body to eat again after a 20 hour fast. Here are some ideas for your breakfast meal:

- Egg and vegetable frittata. If you need to add oil, use coconut oil or avocado oil. Use a variety of vegetables to give you some different vitamins. You could add spinach, broccoli, and bell peppers. Or tomatoes, onions, and garlic. It will be delicious either way. Add a side of fruit, or a side salad to complete the meal.

- Bacon and eggs — a classic American breakfast. Bacon is allowed in the paleo diet and can provide needed flavor to any meal. Use the bacon fat to cook your eggs or discard the fat and cook your eggs in olive oil.

- Hard-boiled eggs with a cooked spinach and bacon salad. Since this is cooked, it's not really a salad, but it is quite delicious. Add some chives or onions for additional flavor.

If none of these appeal to you, you could always find some other recipes online. Fruits and vegetables are always a good breakfast option. A fruit salad with sunflower seeds can be a perfect break from eating eggs in the morning.

Lunch and dinner ideas

Because you only have a small eating window in the warrior diet, it's hard to really have three large meals. It's more likely that you'll have two meals, or just graze during the four hours. So, in this section lunch and dinner are combined. There will also be some recommendations for 'grazing,' or eating small bits consistently. Whichever path you choose, there are a lot of good food options following a paleo diet.

- Chicken salad and grapes. This may sound a little strange, but chicken salad is wonderful with grapes. You can even add some nuts with it for added texture. If you're eating a paleo version with grains, then having some whole-grain toast with the chicken salad.

- Egg salad. In case you're not bored with eggs, then egg salad can be a delicious meal. Add salsa or guacamole to add some flavor. A side salad can provide some additional nutrients and help you remain full.

- Burgers wrapped in lettuce or without any wrapping. Burgers are a great meal. You just can't eat the bun when following the paleo diet.

However, if you want to add grains to your meal, then choose a whole wheat bread with your burger. Whether you have a bun or not, add onions, and other vegetables to your burger. If you want to add something with an amazing taste, then dry some tomatoes in the oven and add them to your burger. Dried tomatoes have an intense flavor which can add something to your meals.

• Salmon and vegetables. Grilled or fried salmon is a great nutrient full meal. Add a side of cooked leafy greens like chard, spinach or arugula to add more nutrients. The fiber from the vegetables can help you remain full during your fasting period.

• Grilled chicken and salsa. Sliced grilled chicken and salsa served on a bed of vegetables can stand in for eating fajitas. Some vegetable options could be grilled onions and peppers, or something like asparagus.

• Steak stir-fry. This can be served with rice, if you're allowing grains as a part of your diet. Choose a steak that you can thinly slice and won't be tough when you cook it. Also slice up some vegetables for your stir fry. Zucchini, asparagus, and corn are good options. Cook it all in coconut oil. Added coconut aminos can give you nice flavor.

• Fresh rolls wrapped in rice 'paper.' This only works if you're allowing grains in your diet. But you can have Vietnamese style fresh rolls that are all wrapped in rice paper. Add some vegetables like peppers and cucumbers to the wrap and top with fish, and an avocado, then wrap it all up.

• Steak with sweet potatoes. This will be very filling. Having sweet potatoes with steak will give you a good mix of protein and fiber, without having to rely on grains. You can do the same combination with chicken and roasted potatoes or fish and potatoes. Add a side salad with arugula for a bit of spice.

If you want to eat constantly during your four hours, instead of having a large meal, then choose items that are whole and unprocessed. Here are some ideas:

• Raw fruits. Nearly any fruit is edible on the paleo diet. So, eat the ones you love the most. You should eat a lot of fruits and vegetables to give you the necessary fiber for your diet.

- Raw vegetables. Just choose the ones you like! Most vegetables are allowed on the paleo diet. Just don't eat legumes like beans and lentils.

- Nuts like pistachios, pecans, and almonds. Most nuts are welcome in a paleo diet, but some are not. Peanuts for example are classified as a legume, so they can't be eaten on a paleo diet.

- Seeds like pumpkin seeds, sunflower seeds, and flax seeds. Seeds are a great snack. You can even turn them into a dessert. You can mix chia seeds, honey, and coconut milk for a delicious 'pudding.' The chia seeds soak up the milk and turn gelatinous, creating a nice dessert.

- Trail mix. Mix up some trail mix with seeds, nuts, and a little chocolate. Dark chocolate that is 70% cocoa is paleo and can give you that little bit of sweetness you're missing.

- Meat or Plant-based Jerky. If you like salty foods, then jerky can be a good paleo option. Just make sure you drink enough water to make up for the salt.

- Hard boiled eggs. Yes, here they are again. Eggs are excellent foods for snacking!

- While on the warrior diet, you can eat paleo foods or just follow a regularwell-balanced meal. Either way, you'll only have four hours to eat all your required calories, so make sure your meals are nutritious.

Maintaining Well-Balanced Meals

When following a fast, it's important that you're getting the right nutrition, as I've mentioned several times before. If you don't want to follow a specific diet, then aim for healthy, wholesome foods. A good way of doing this is having a well-balanced meal. Most of us have learned what a healthy meal constitutes in school. It was drilled into us during health class, possibly pointed to in biology class, and repeatedly mentioned by the school nurse. But most of us don't eat well-balanced meals. We instead eat what's convenient. With so many easy to find restaurants, food can be at our fingertips. Most of that food isn't healthy, and while it can be difficult for some Americans to find healthy foods, if you have them available to you, then choose wholesome foods, rather than fast foods.

If you have difficulty figuring out what makes a well-balanced meal, you can explore some of the resources provided by the U.S. Health Department. They even have a website dedicated to showing how to portion your meals and include all the food groups during your day. The website can offer you customizable meal plans that will give you nutritious meals and can provide other resources so that you can make the best meal decisions for your body type.

When you have a well-balanced meal, it means that you're eating a bit from at least three different food groups. The food groups are fruits, vegetables, grains, proteins, and dairy.

Fruit is...well...fruit. It's self-explanatory. While you want to eat some fruit each day, you're not going to eat as much as you do vegetables. Fruits can be high in sugar, so choose fruits that aren't as high and eat those more frequently. Try a variety of different kinds of fruit because they can each contain different vitamins and nutrients. So, pick and choose, and don't stick with the same fruit every day. Despite what they say, an apple a day doesn't keep the doctor away. Instead, mix up your fruit choices. The vegetable family includes a lot of variety. Think pumpkins, corn, broccoli, onions, and beans. All of these are part of the vegetable group. They're also one of the largest families of food you should eat during your day. In general, at least one-third or half of your plate should be vegetables. Just like with fruit, you want to mix up your vegetables because they each provide a different type and number of vitamins. For example, yellow pumpkins can give you way more vitamin A than many other veggies. So, mix it up.

Grains are a large food group and the family consists of food produced by a grain plant. Some grain plants include wheat, bran, rye, rice, oats, and sometimes corn. All of this is then processed into other foods like bread, oatmeal, polenta, tortilla's, cereal, etc. All of these are a part of the grain food family. Grains should also be a large part of your meal. About one third of your plate will be grains. Whole grains are a better option than other types. Think whole-wheat bread vs. white bread. Choose brown rice over white rice. These types of grain contain more nutrients.

The protein family has a variety of different items in it. It can contain lean meats that are unprocessed, seafood, beans, nuts, and tofu. Some lean meats are lamb, beef, and pork. Sausages, hot dogs, and salami are considered processed and less healthy. You should eat these only in small quantities. But lean meat itself is quite healthy and you should eat about seven servings in a week. Seafood is another great choice and you should have at least two servings in your week. Seafood includes fish, shrimp, scallops, octopus, etc. Beans, nuts, and tofu are other kinds of protein. They are all plant based and are excellent alternatives to meat or seafood. You should try to have some meatless/plant-based foods during your week and beans can give you an alternative that will keep you full.

The dairy family is our last food group. It consists of animal products like milk, eggs, cheese, and yogurt. When you choose a dairy item, it should be a low-fat variety. Full fat yogurt can be very healthy and provide you with essential vitamins and probiotics.

Dairy should only be a small percentage of your daily dietary consumption.

When choosing well-balanced meals, try to avoid heavily processed foods and fast foods. These can be full of sugar, carbs, and fats that aren't healthy for you. However, eating out every now and again is completely fine. Just don't make it a daily habit. Other foods like processed meats, alcohol, fatty foods, and 'junk' foods should be limited so that they do not take up a huge portion of your weekly eating.

While you fast, you want your food choices to give you the best balance of nutrients. So, following a well-balanced meal will help you maintain your weight, or even promote weight loss depending on what your diet was like before you started fasting. While you could eat all the right nutrients, you might still be sabotaging yourself with your portion sizes. So be aware of the portion size as well as the nutrients in each of your meals. Below, we'll explore some possible meal ideas that are well-balanced.

Breakfast ideas

When you break your fast, try to eat a combination of protein and fiber to keep you full. It will also help you recover, if you decided to work out before fasting. Make sure that your keeping a record of what you eat so that you can check to see how your body responds to different foods after a long fasting period. Some people can have a negative reaction to eating certain foods after breaking their fast, so stay mindful about what you're eating and check in with yourself regularly to see if you're reacting badly to something you ate. Here are some great well-balanced breakfast ideas.

• Whole-grain English muffins with eggs, butter, and spinach. Add a side of fruit like mixed berries or a banana. This meal covers four food groups: grains, protein, dairy, and vegetables.

• Oatmeal with sunflower seeds, diced apple, and a bit of yogurt. This meal has items from four food groups. The yogurt is your protein, and the oatmeal is your fiber and grain. So, this meal will keep you fuller than just eating toast alone.

• Whole grain bread with peanut butter or a nut butter alternative. Add some fruit on the side or on the sandwich itself. Consider blueberries on top of peanut butter and toast. Or bananas. Bananas and peanut butter are magic.

• Yogurt with fruit, nuts, and some crumbled granola. This meal provides you four different food groups. This is heavier in dairy, so you would want to have less dairy in the rest of your day. Alternatively, you can substitute dairy for non-dairy milk options as well if you are dairy intolerant. Increase how much fruit you add if you want to have a fiber rich breakfast.

• Cheese omelet with diced peppers, onions, and broccoli. Eat it with a sideof toast if you want to add a grain.

A lot of the meals listed here have items from four food groups. You don't have to do that for your meals. These are just recommendations. In general, just make sure you combine a protein and fiber to keep you full. An example would be having Raisin Bran cereal (fiber) with a cup of 2% milk (protein). Lunch ideas

With lunch, try to make a good portion of your meal vegetables. This will help you meet your daily vegetable serving and give you a good amount of nutrients and vitamins. A good option is having a salad for lunch, but this can be unwilling. So, add some protein and one other food group. All of this can help you have a satisfying lunch while fasting.

Here are some lunch ideas.

• Cobb salad with a mix of leafy greens, roasted beets, tomatoes, crumbled blue cheese, and hard-boiled eggs. If you don't want to eat eggs with your lunch, substitute them for canned beans. Black beans and roasted chickpeas are good alternatives.

• Shrimp bowl with brown rice, lime flavored shrimp, sliced tomatoes, and avocado salsa. This meal provides you with your protein and fiber. It also gives you some tasty foods with avocado salsa and lime-flavored shrimp. If you're warming it up at work, check in with your coworkers, just in case the scent of seafood is off putting for anyone else around the office.

• Roasted chicken, with arugula salad and roasted new potatoes. This meal is one that you could also have for dinner. You could bring the leftovers for lunch. Whichever way, it will be filling and be a tasty alternative to eating out for lunch.

• Jacket sweet potato with corn salsa, sour cream, and black beans. This vegetarian lunch provides you with a lot of protein from the beans and sour cream. If you don't want to eat sour cream, then replace it with plain Greek yogurt.

• Five bean chilies. This will have a lot of protein and fiber from the beans, as well as a good amount of vegetables from the tomatoes, onions, and garlic in the chili.

If these don't appeal to you, then find some recipes online that look interesting. Don't feel limited by what's listed here. There are so many recipes out there that can help you choose healthy options while also being very delicious. Take some time to pick out some things you can cook and eat during the week. This will make your fasting easier if you already have your meals planned out.

Dinner ideas

This is usually your last meal before your fast. So, you want to make it very nutritious and something that will help tide you over your fasting period. If you're going to bed immediately after eating, then choose things that aren't going to disrupt your sleep. Some people feel like dairy before bed gives them nightmares, so if you're one of those people, skip dairy in your dinner. If you're having disrupted sleep but don't know the cause, then check your food journal. What did you eat before bed every night? Perhaps the problem is there. Or perhaps the problem is elsewhere. Having a record of your food choices can help you make the best decisions for your health.

To make your meal planning easier, make enough dinner to bring the extras for lunch the next day. This can help you make fasting easier. You could also plan your meals for the week on the weekends, then spend your time cooking them during your weekend. This way, all your meals are already prepared, and you just must reach into the fridge for one type to eat. Having your meals planned out will help you while you're fasting. It will also reduce and feelings of food obsession, since you'll already have things prepared and won't be constantly thinking of other foods. Here are some well-balanced meal ideas:

• Beef and cheese lasagna. Add vegetables in between the layers for added nutrients. Some great options are sliced eggplant, roasted red peppers, even some spinach. All of them can add to the value of your meal. If this doesn't appeal to you, then eat the lasagna with a side salad, using a variety of vegetables. Keep your portions small since lasagna can have a lot of cheese in it.

• Steamed trout with a side of new potatoes and swiss chard. This is one of my favorite meals. Trout is delicious and full of good antioxidants. It also tends to be less expensive than salmon, making it affordable and accessible. Swiss chard is bitter, and some people don't like it. If it's not your cup of tea, then replace it with other leafy vegetables like collard greens or kale.

• Chicken curry with potatoes and green peas. Depending on how you make your curry sauce, you should have a lot of vegetables already in the curry itself. The spices in curry are very good for you and can provide a lot of nutrients.

• Pumpkin soup with cashews and coconut milk. This is honestly divine. You'll get your protein from the coconut milk and cashews, with the fiber from the pumpkin. It's very smooth and decadent. If this flavor profile isn't for you, try it with chicken broth replacing the coconut milk, and crumbled bacon replacing the cashews. As some thyme to taste.

• Slow-cooked shredded pork tacos. Use roasted pineapple in the tacos andadd thinly sliced vegetables like radishes or lettuce. Choose whole wheat or corn tortillas to wrap your tacos, and top with salsa or guacamole.

Try to have at least a couple servings of fish in your week and consider some meatless meals. Eating too much meat is not very healthy, so mix it up.

Replace some meat in your favorite recipes with tofu or beans instead.

To conclude this chapter, all these different kinds of foods and meals can help you be successful with your intermittent fast. Choose the type of diet you want to follow for your fast, or don't change your diet at all. The choice is entirely up to you. If you notice that you're gaining weight while on the fast, then look at your diet. It may be the problem. If you're not satisfied with what you're currently eating on your fast, then change your diet! For people who are not following the 5:2 or alternative day method, try to maintain a diet that has at least 1,300 calories during your days. Otherwise you'll be in danger of becoming malnourished. Good luck with your meals on the fast!

Chapter 07
Motivation to Stick with Your Plan

I wish I could tell you that fasting is all sunshine and roses. I wish I could tell you that it's so easy to follow. Unfortunately, it's not. There are going to be days when you look at your cup of coffee and cry because you can't eat anything for another four hours. There are going to be days when you throw yourself at the doors of the local cafe and ogle all the pastries and lattes, knowing that by the time you can eat, the doors will be closed. There will be days when all your friends are out drinking and partying, and your eating window just ended. Basically, there are going to be frustrating days, sad days, difficult days, stressful days, and nightmare days where you're going to want to throw in the towel and give up on your fast. These are the kinds of days that you'll need motivation to help you continue your fast. Without the motivation, it's likely that you'll end your fasting period early, not start the next fasting period, or just give up all together.

One key thing you can do to keep yourself motivated is to remind yourself of the days that were amazing. Think about that day last week, when you had your latte and your boss didn't yell at you. Think about that morning, when your dogs lovingly jumped on the bed and woke you up with millions of kisses. Think about that time that you dropped your scarf on the train and someone found it and returned it to you. The recollection of these good days can help remind you that your days will get better. You can use these reminders on the rough days when you just want to give up on fasting, or the days when you just want to sit on the bathroom floor and cry. When your days are rough and you have the stress of fasting on top of that, it's likely that you'll break your fast. However, it's important that you continue your fast again in the future, even if you hit some speed bumps along the way. This chapter will cover some points that may help you continue to feel motivated.

Distract Yourself

Sometimes the hunger that comes with fasting can be overwhelming. This is especially true with fasts that require 24 hours of not eating. If you can't seem to stop thinking about food, or if you're just feeling gnawing hunger, then you might want to break your fast early and just eat everything in front of you. Before doing that, see if some distractions will help you maintain your fasts. Some good distractions include work, exercise, and meditation. Work probably shouldn't be classified as a distraction, but it can be a useful one when you're fasting. Having your mind occupied by something that requires you to be actively engaged is a great way to distract yourself from your feelings of hunger. Many of us have already experienced this. If you've ever been in the 'flow' while working, you've probably skipped meals without realizing it. You may have even come out of flow and realized that hours have gone by and your stomach is growling at you. This realization can help you when you're fasting. You can try to get into a state of flow, but if that is beyond you at that moment, then just get engaged with work. Start a new project or plan. If your work is very active, then get fully engaged with the activity. If your work is passive, then find another way to distract yourself.

One way of distracting yourself is to do some light exercises. Depending on the fast you're following, heavy exercise might be too much. Light exercises on the other hand, can be a great distraction and won't affect you negatively. Light exercises include things like walking and yoga. They aren't high intensity and don't involve too much effort on your part. So, they shouldn't cause you to feel nauseous or faint. Walking outside in nature is a perfect distraction. Instead of walking and focusing on your hunger, focus on things outside of you. Look at the trees, birds, and insects. Observe the other people around you, breathe in deeply, and just walk. Allow your mind to wander, but if it keeps going to your hunger, then refocus on something else. Yoga is another way that you can distract yourself. Because it requires more focus on the positions and your breath, you will quickly find yourself distracted from your hunger.

Use your distractions wisely. While it's okay to distract yourself from feeling hungry, it's not okay to distract yourself from feeling intensely uncomfortable. If you're feeling unwell, then this is a sign to step back from the fast and speak to a doctor. Don't "power through" something that isn't working for you.

Remind Yourself of Your Goals

When you fast, you usually have reasons for why you are choosing to do it. Maybe your goal is to lose weight, maybe it's just gone get healthier in general. Your goals should be personal to you, not something that's mimicry of other people's goals. Think about why you really want to fast. Think about a goal that will really motivate you to continue fasting. Whatever your reasoning, your goals can help you maintain motivation. To help you remember your goals, write them down. You can put them in the same journal you put your food notes in, or you can make a specific fasting journal with your fasting schedule, food notes, and goals all together. Having them written down makes them more concrete and gives you something to look back on when your fast becomes difficult to sustain.

As you start to feel weary of continuing your fast, or if you struggle with the hours without food, then take the time to say your goals. Write them down somewhere so you see them frequently. You can use a dry erase marker and put your goals on your bathroom mirror. That way every day as you start your eating window you can see your goals, and every evening as you bring your eating window to a close, you're reminded of why you're fasting. During the day, when you struggle with your fast, take a moment to repeat your goals to yourself. You can say it like a mantra to help you stay focused and ignore the hunger.

Beyond repeating your goals to yourself, you can create a visual to help embody your goals. You can create a vision board. A lot of people create these boards to help remind them of their goals in many aspects of their lives. Usually, it's created with cutouts from magazines or printed pictures. Each image represents something specifically to you. If your goal is to buy a house, then you might have a picture of a beautiful house. For fasting, if your goal is to be healthier, then your picture can be anything that embodies the word 'health' to you. It could be people exercising, or even just a mountain with clean air. Your images are unique to you. Once you have your goal images, put them together in a collage and post them somewhere that you'll see your vision board every day. Your office or kitchen, maybe your bedroom, are all good choices.

Finally, if fasting is really getting you down and you don't have your vision board or written goals near at hand, then do a visualization technique. Close your eyes and in your mind, visualize yourself as you have reached your goal. What do you look like? What emotions do you feel? How do you feel physically? How do you feel mentally? Consider all these questions to help you visualize your goal achievement. This can help you remain motivated to fasting, and give you the encouragement to keep going, even after you've broken your fast.

Be Compassionate Towards Yourself

Have you ever notices that the closer we are to someone, the harsher we are to them? Like, our acquaintances see us as these perfect angels, but our friends know that we have a sharp wit, and an even sharper tongue. Our family knows that we don't take no nonsense from anyone and our family gets a big brunt of our anger when we feel miserable. But the person we treat the worst is ourselves. Any slight failure or disillusionment results in us reprimanding ourselves. Comments like, "I'm so stupid" or "Why am I such an idiot?" are things that we say to ourselves. We would never say them to our friends or acquaintances. So, we're insanely harsh to ourselves.

When to hit a snag with fasting, maybe cheat a little with what we eat or skip a fasting period, it's not uncommon for us to have some selfrecriminating thoughts. These thoughts aren't beneficial. They often tear us down without providing an area to build ourselves up again. They can be extremely negative and result in us giving up our fasts all together. Instead of sulking with our own thoughts and giving up on our fasts, we should try to practice a little self-kindness.

What would you say to a friend who said they failed at their fast and they're so stupid? Would you agree with them? That's unlikely. It's more likely that you'll try to console them, reassure them that they aren't stupid, and follow up by encouraging them to continue trying. Do the same thing that you would do for a friend but do it for yourself. Instead of saying, "I'm so stupid, I failed," say, "I took a cheat day, and that's okay. I'll get right back into my fasting schedule." Be positive and compassionate towards yourself. We all make mistakes and we all have lapses. Simply learn from your experience, adapt your fasting schedule to accommodate what you've learned, and start fasting again. Don't give up just because of a little bump in the road.

Get Some Support + Bonus 16/8 method

Things are always easier with support. Some of us like to think that we're eagles, living solo among all the turkeys. We want to be free without anyone there to back us up. We don't need them! But this isn't ideal, especially when things are difficult. Sometimes, it's better to be surrounded by turkeys who care about you and will support you. Sometimes it's better to be the turkey because you know you're lovingly supported by your friends and family with you. What I'm trying to say here is that when you struggle with intermittent fasting, having the support of your friends can really make a difference in your success or failure.

If you have some friends who are very supportive of you, make sure they know when you're struggling with your fasting goals. They can probably give you a good shoulder to cry on and may even give you some tips for how to make things easier. If you're very lucky, your friends may join your fast with you. This way, you can keep each other accountable. If they don't want to fast, that's okay too so long as they're supportive of you following your health goals. If you're truly an eagle, alone in the world, then seek support from online communities. There are a lot of blogs and forums out there, dedicated to intermittent fasting. Join some of them and talk to others who are struggling. Some great forums to join include the Reddit forum on intermittent fasting. There, they post pictures of success, questions about speed bumps, and even give each other motivation. Get involved and you'll have some support too.

To conclude this chapter, fasting is hard, but it can be done with the right support behind you and the motivation to push forward. Keep persevering, keep trying, and only give up if your body can't handle the fast. Even when you make a mistake or take a cheat day (or month), just try again when you're ready. Keep trying. Explore what it is, why it works, and who it's for. We'll also discuss a step-by-step approach for starting the 16/8 method, whether you are a beginner faster or have been fasting with other methods for a while. We'll investigate how to fast in combination with different diets and whether it should be done. Finally, we'll also cover exercising while fasting and troubleshooting some issues that may come up while fasting.

It's important to note that when using the term "fasting" in this book, we are talking specifically about intermittent fasting, not other kinds. Starting a new fasting program is an exciting time, and we're glad you're reading this book to help you with the process. When you're ready, let's begin!

Chapter 08: Chapter bonus: Fasting

Overview of the 16/8 Method

The 16/8 method of intermittent fasting gets a lot of press. It's the type of fasting that many celebrities do to get in shape for a movie. It's also considered one of the most natural methods of fasting because it doesn't require calorie counting or drastic changes. It's easy to understand why it's so popular when fasting, in conjunction with proper nutrition and exercise, can result in weight loss. However, the 16/8 method is more than just a tool for weight loss. It is a tool for overall better health.

Intermittent fasting with the 16/8 method is not a diet. It's not about restricting your calories or denying your body of a key food group. It's just about scheduling the right times to eat in your day. If you want to expand your fast to include a specific diet, you can always do that, but the fast itself is not a diet. When following the 16/8 method, you are choosing to fast for 16 hours and eat during an eight-hour period. All your meals must be during the eight hours, and there shouldn't be any snacking outside of it. During the 16 hours of fast, you can drink water, tea, and coffee, though a lot of people say that you should not have caffeine while fasting since that can disturb your sleep later. Others say that caffeine can help curb your appetite, so you will have to choose what you want to drink based on how it affects your body.

The 16/8 method is a simple way to ease into fasting because it merely involves either having a later breakfast or an early dinner on your fasting days. If you're sleeping a full eight hours, then you've already completed eight hours of the fast! This is one of the positive aspects of the 16/8 method. Because it also doesn't require you to change your diet (though that's recommended), you don't have to make a considerable change. If you've read any articles about New Year's resolutions, then you'll know that failure is inevitable when making massive changes to your habits. It's easier to make a change to your habits if it's a smaller change. Because the 16/8 method is convenient, it's a small enough habit to take on.

In general, the 16/8 method doesn't require you to follow a new diet. To reap the most rewards from the fast, reducing your processed foods and sugars can help provide you with more benefits. If you want to increase the chances of weight loss, you can always combine fasting with the diet of your choice. However, that isn't required, and you should get your doctor's approval before combining intermittent fasting and dieting.

There are a lot of benefits to following the 16/8 method of fasting. While there is research to support this style of fasting, there still needs to be more research completed to prove the efficacy of this method with humans. In the few studies out there, researchers have found that fasting can bring about a lot of positive physiological changes. It has been shown to improve insulin resistance, metabolism, and cardiovascular health. It can also reduce your weight, blood pressure, and the likelihood of diseases like diabetes. Fasting for a more extended period than your usual sleep time results in more opportunities for your body to heal itself. After all, much of your energy goes into running your digestive tract. Yet if you haven't eaten, then your energy goes into other things like healing. This happens every night as you sleep.

While all the previous benefits mentioned are amazing, they're not something that you can physically see or feel, except for weight loss. One advantage of fasting that you will be able to feel is reduced cravings and even a decreased appetite. Most of this is anecdotal since it's hard to measure cravings and hunger, but many people say that they feel fuller longer while following the 16/8 method. Even better, their cravings for empty calories, sugars, and carbs were also reduced. This means that they didn't eat as many foods that cause weight gain and instead ate more food that was healthier and more nutritious.

With every positive mentioned for fasting, it is also essential to explain the drawbacks. Again, since there isn't a large body of research dedicated to the 16/8 method, these drawbacks still need to be researched. When starting a fast, some people will feel dizziness or a change in their sleep patterns. On the fast, it's important to be mindful of the way your body is feeling. If you are having disrupted sleep, feel dizzy, or even feel bloated, reevaluate your fasting. Everyone will react differently, so it's important to talk to your doctor about the risks associated with intermittent fasts before you start one. Another drawback includes midday hunger. We've all been there. We're at work, typing away, and it's been too long since we last ate. Every error or slight causes us frustration. This is commonly known as being hangry, or hungry and angry. If your fast isn't timed right, or if your meals aren't providing enough for you, then you might feel hangry. To prevent this drawback, it's necessary to time your meals right and ensure that you are eating robust, well-balanced, nutritious meals. If you decide to break your fast with gummy worms at 10:00 a.m., then expect to feel seriously hungry within a couple of hours. Just try not to take your "hanger" out on your coworkers.

Binge eating is another possible drawback to fasting for 16 hours. You may have experienced this in the past after forgetting a meal. After being hungry for a while, we tend to eat more to overcompensate for our temporary starvation. This can put us into a feast-fast pattern, which isn't good for your body. It floods it with too many calories at once, and most of them won't be healthy. Let's be honest, you aren't going to be binging on carrot sticks. Instead, it will be chips and chocolate. Binging is obviously not healthy and won't provide you with the necessary nutrition to continue your fast. Instead of binging, it's essential to time your meals. You don't want to be so hungry that you start gorging on everything in your pantry. This will reverse any positive effects that fasting can do for you and will cause you to gain weight. So, plan the time of your meals and what you're going to eat. Control the portions, and again, eat a hearty, well-balanced meal.

From a medical standpoint, there have been some risks associated with women fasting. With animal studies, researchers found that some mice had reduced fertility due to the eating restrictions/ energy timing from intermittent fasting (Kumar & Kaur, 2013). While this hasn't carried over into human studies, some women have reported changed menstruation cycles and missed periods. So, women must talk to their doctor before fasting, especially if they are taking fertility treatments or if they have experienced amenorrhea before.

A final drawback, which may be a serious one, depending on what you like, is that there can be a social impact when fasting. It's very common for people to want to go out with friends and family, eat out, celebrate birthdays with too much beer or cake, etc. However, when you have a fasting schedule, your outings may not fit within it. This can be a huge drawback for some people. You could, of course, choose not to fast on days when you want to eat out with friends and family, but this could disrupt your cycle and result in some uncomfortable symptoms. You can adjust your fasting cycle as you see fit.

Some people follow the 16/8 pattern every day, but many choose only to follow it a couple of days a week or only one day a week. So, you can decide how you want to fast and even choose to take specific days off to eat with your friends.

There are some benefits and drawbacks to following the 16/8 method of intermittent fasting. However, it's still a great way to work on improving your body and your understanding of how you eat.

Why It Works

There are a lot of studies about intermittent fasting and why it works. Most of these studies are with animal subjects like monkeys and rats. While these animals are closely related in physiology to humans, there are enough differences that more human studies need to be conducted. The few studies that focus on human participants do show some promise. They show persistent reasons why intermittent fasting can work for humans as a way to become healthier. The 16/8 method works precisely because of its connection to your circadian rhythm. It also works because of unplanned caloric restriction and gives your body time to burn stored fat. All these factors work together to create a habit that can reset your physiology and improve your resistance to sickness and weight gain. Circadian Rhythms

The circadian rhythm is your body's natural reaction to light and darkness. It's what promotes your sleep habits, changes your metabolism, and even affects your behavior. Your hormones change according to your circadian rhythm, and so do your eating habits. Because the circadian rhythm has helped us evolve, it forces us into a natural fasting/eating period within 24 hours. It is also why you tend to want to be awake during the day and asleep during the night so you can rest and heal at night and eat during the daylight.

Of course, we mess around with the rhythm somewhat regularly as we get too little sleep, stay awake late, skip meals, or drink coffee in the middle of the day. All of this disrupts our circadian rhythm. Disturbing our circadian rhythm is now considered the new norm in our culture. However, our bodies have yet to catch up and evolve to this new norm. We're still stuck in the past, where having energy in the morning was more important than having it in the evening. Since our bodies haven't changed much, having a disrupted circadian rhythm can shake up our equilibrium. It can cause sleep disorders like insomnia, diseases like diabetes and obesity, and mental health issues like manic and depressive episodes. The importance of the circadian rhythm cannot be understated.

Now you might be wondering what fasting has to do with our sleep cycle, but I guarantee there is a connection. This is because our circadian rhythm not only dictates the times when we are asleep or awake but also dictates when our metabolism is most functional and when it slows down. When we match this rhythm to an eating/fasting schedule, it can reduce our risk for heart attack, stroke, and diabetes (Amnesia et al., 2018).

The circadian rhythm tells our body when to eat, store food, and utilize the stores of food during a fast. It tells our bodies to seek nourishment when it is light outside. We store food once we have eaten enough to survive, and it tells us to use the food stores we have when asleep at night. Nighttime is when our body uses its food stores and starts healing damaged cells. While fasting, the body goes into a healing mode so that once the light is available again, we have enough energy to find more food. However, most of us tend not to leave a long enough fasting time and instead eat regularly and often. This changes our physiology and reduces the time our body must heal itself. Eating frequently without a long period of rest can cause changes and disruptions in our hormone levels. It can also reduce the amount of cellular repair that usually occurs during our fasting time. This imbalance can throw our circadian rhythm out of its cycle. Having a regular pattern of eating/resting with a long enough fasting time can restore the rhythm and help to reverse any damage done (Manoogian & Panda, 2016). Overall, while doing intermittent fasting, especially while following the 16/8 method, you're going to be following your natural circadian rhythm. This can help improve your hormone levels, your metabolism, and how your cells regenerate. By utilizing something that is already well established in your body, your circadian cycle, you're adding oomph to your dietary goals. All of this can improve your overall health, which is why intermittent fasting works.

Caloric Restriction

Another reason why the 16/8 method works is that it results in caloric restriction, even if that isn't your intention. Because you have such a small window of time to eat, many people can't eat as much as they used to. This is, of course, anecdotal, but many people say that while fasting, they usually can't eat as much as they used to. Even if they eat two large meals in the day and some snacks, they aren't eating as much because the meals must be pretty big to have the same caloric value as three meals. Because they're not making up those calories, they're consuming fewer calories than when they used to have the same meals and snacks throughout the day. Calorie restriction isn't surprising when you realize that you can't eat that much food within eight hours. You're going to be full, so for the most part, you are going to be reducing your calorie intake.

If you want some proof from research, then here it is. In a study by Gill and Panda, participants ate their meals in a 10-hour window and had a 20% reduction in calorie consumption (as cited in Longo & Panda, 2017). A lot of people unintentionally overeat within 24 hours. We just like to keep snacking in between our large meals and even eat way into the night. But when we're fasting, we tend to reduce how much we eat because it's such a short period of time to eat our meals. We feel full longer and don't have the same time to have cravings like we used to. Because the participants were unintentionally eating less, they lost some weight, about 4% of their body weight, and kept it off for a year (as cited in Longo & Panda, 2017). Those results are great. While these participants didn't follow the 16/8 fasting method, they did do a similar fast where they fasted for 14 hours and ate during a 10-hour period. The results of this are promising. It's important to note that caloric restriction was not the goal of the fast. The fast itself was the goal, and the result was weight loss. This worked because of unplanned caloric restriction.

Obviously, one thing that won't help this is binging when your hungry right after your fast. If you just keep consuming food without thought, you won't have any caloric restriction, and your fasting won't work for you. To prevent this, time out your meals during your fast. Many people choose to eat a small breakfast and then two large meals for lunch and dinner. These last two meals can keep you full while you do the final hours of your fast before bed. By timing out your meals, you can gain the benefits of unplanned caloric restriction and reduce the chances of binging. In the next couple of chapters, we'll go over potential schedules for eating so that you won't feel hungry while you fast. Burning Stored Fat

There are many reasons why the 16/8 method works, but we're going to cover just one more. The 16/8 method helps your body burn more stored fat for energy. Generally, as we eat consistently, our body is converting the food into sugars and fats that it then uses to power our day. However, because we eat a lot, the extra sugars and fats get stored away in preparation for a "starvation" event, when we won't have food. It's an evolutionary result that came about from our ancestors and times when food was scarce. However, we don't really have the problem of food scarcity anymore in the Western world. In fact, we tend to eat more than we need, and our food is also higher in sugars and fats. This means that we're storing more than we're using. And as we keep continually eating, we then keep storing instead of using the stores that we have.

Now, most people know that you can use exercise to help this problem. Exercise uses the energy the food is providing us and uses the stores of fat to continue energizing us. Exercise is a way to burn off the fat, but many people are unaware that fasting is too. Fasting works because it gives you a period where you aren't eating. This makes your body use some of your stores to keep energizing you. With nothing coming in, your body stops storing extra fat and instead starts using your stores (Tello, 2018). The fast gives your body the chance to use what it already has at its disposal. That's why fasting works to become healthier and lose weight.

Who Shouldn't Try It?

"Intermittent fasting is for everyone! Go now and fast!" is probably what you want us to say, but unfortunately, we can't say that. Fasting with the 16/8 method works for some people, but not all.

Let's go over the people who should and shouldn't try intermittent fasting.

If you are relatively healthy and you just want to try something new, go ahead and try intermittent fasting with the 16/8 method. This is especially true if you are already familiar with healthy habits like exercising and eating balanced meals. You're already equipped with the knowledge necessary to achieve your goals with fasting. Before jumping into a new fasting program, examine your current health and lifestyle. Here are some things for you to consider before trying the 16/8 method:

1.   1. If you have a family, think about how you're going to plan your meals.When will you eat your last meal? What will you eat? Will your partner be involved with fasting too? Do you have the necessary resolve to cook for and feed your children while you are fasting?

2.   2. Consider the possible ups and downs you may experience as you start your fasting journey. You may have some shifts in your mood and possibly your sleeping habits. Will these disrupt your life a lot? How can you combat these shifts or prepare people around you for these shifts?

3.   3. Do you have a support system who can help you? You can do intermittent fasting without a support system, but honestly, goals are easier to achieve if you have people cheering for you. These people can be your friends, family, or even your pets! So long as you have support, things will be more comfortable.

4.   4. If you are in athletics and sports, it's highly recommended you talk to your doctor and coach before fasting. Fasting can work for you, but you'll need to change your protein intake. You don't want to have lows while doing your athletic feats. Dropping like flies while playing soccer is not a goal anyone wants, so work with your doctor, dietitian, or coach before starting a fast.

Most of us can work with intermittent fasting without having to struggle too much. However, some people should not be fasting unless their doctor prescribes it. This includes those who are pregnant, have eating disorders, have medical complications, and of course, children. Let's investigate this further.

Pregnant Women

If you're eating for two, you should not be skipping meals. Unless your doctor says that you must fast, please don't. At this stage of your health and your baby's development, you need to take the right balance of nutrients and calories. Fasting can mess with this. Beyond this, while pregnant, there are often vitamins and additional medications that need to be taken. Many of these need to be taken with food. Fasting can make this difficult. Finally, with pregnancy comes hormone changes. Fasting also causes some hormone changes (as mentioned in the section about circadian rhythm). You don't want to be adding additional stress to your body because it's already changing to accommodate the baby. So please don't fast until your baby is weaned and you're both happy and healthy.

People with Medical and Mental Illness

So, the first mental illness we're going to cover is eating disorders because they are all about what you eat and how you think about food. They can be challenging to overcome. Generally, there are three eating disorders: anorexia, bulimia, and binge eating. All of these represent difficulty with food and the person's relationship with food. Anorexia and fasting should not mix. Anorexia is, essentially, starvation and results in significant malnourishment. If you have a history of anorexia, you shouldn't fast. Starting a fast can cause you to relapse into anorexia instead of keeping a healthy eating/resting schedule. If you experience bulimia and binging, you also should not be fasting. Again, all these eating disorders represent a misunderstanding of the purpose of food to our health and well-being. Fasting restricts what you eat and can cause you to relapse into an eating disorder if you already have a history of one. So please do not pursue fasting if you previously had an eating disorder.

Other Mental Illness

In general, if you're struggling with a mental illness, it's essential that you work on that and on your physical well-being without stressing your body with a fast. Fasting does cause some stress, but most importantly, it can also cause some hormonal changes. These can affect your mental health if you're already struggling. Beyond just the struggle with hormone changes, if you're being treated for a mental illness, you may have to take medications. Many medications shouldn't be taken on an empty stomach or may need to be taken at a specific time of day. This can complicate a fasting schedule. If you're dead set on fasting while working on your mental health, speak with your doctor and psychologist before starting. They'll be able to help you find a way to begin fasting without further endangering your body and mental well-being.

Advanced Diabetes

While fasting can help with insulin resistance, if you already have diabetes, then fasting isn't for you. You shouldn't pursue it until after talking with your doctor. Fasting can cause changes in your insulin levels, metabolic levels, and of course, your glucose levels. This can play life-endangering havoc with your body if you are already struggling with insulin and hormone levels. Please, please, please, speak to your doctor before even approaching fasts. Your doctor will be able to give you a better idea of your body's current state and where you can adjust with your eating without fasting.

Irritable Bowel Syndrome

If you have irritable bowel syndrome, fasting isn't recommended. This is because fasting can impact the way you digest food and how your metabolism works. This can cause some irritation to an already irritable bowel. Some people have experienced bloating while fasting as well. So, speak with your doctor about what you can do with fasting before starting.

In general, if you have a medical condition, you should speak with your doctor before starting any new diet or fast. Your doctor knows what your body can handle, and they can give you recommendations for meeting your dietary goals without risking your health.

Children

It's so easy to be a child or a teenager and feel pressure to look like celebrities do. Girls especially have been taught they have to look away within our society. They may look through social media and find many examples of the perfect body. They may want that body for themselves and choose to control their food and their relationship to food by dieting. However, this is an easy way to slip into disordered eating. Children shouldn't fast. Full stop. Children are using each piece of food they eat to grow and develop their bodies and brains. They are creating a system that works for them, but also creating habits that can be lifelong. Fasting can easily slip into anorexia. It's an easy slope to fall, and children are still learning about their relationship with food and how it makes them feel. If they fast, they may learn to make it a habit that can lead to poor nutrition or even disordered eating, all of which can persist within their adult lives. Children shouldn't fast. If your child or teenager wants to improve their diet, they can do that by choosing healthy options for food, having nutritious meals, and exercising. They don't need to fast to achieve their diet and body goals, and they shouldn't.

To conclude this chapter, intermittent fasting with the 16/8 method has some significant benefits and some drawbacks. It's also not for everyone. So please take the time to analyze your life situation before starting your fast. Also, consider speaking with your doctor if you're unsure about how fasting can help you. Once you are ready to begin, let's head to our next chapter, where we'll explore the step-by-step process of starting your fasting journey.

Chapter 09
Following the 16/8 Method Step-by-Step

We've already covered the basics of the 16/8 method, but here's a reminder. With the 16/8 method, you are fasting for 16 hours and eating within an eight-hour period. You'll have all your meals within these eight hours. Outside of them, have a lot of fluids (water, tea, black coffee) but no food and no sugar in your drinks. Remember, the 16/8 method is not a diet, just a specific time to eat.

Now that you know more about the fast, you may be ready to just jump right in and start! While this is an option, you might want to know more about what to do with the fast. In this chapter, we're going to cover what to do step-by-step. We're going to give you some guidance to transition into the 16/8 method. We'll also talk about what a month-long schedule might look like as you transition into the fast.

Starting from Scratch: Transitioning from No Fast to Fasting

We've talked a lot about the positives of the 16/8 method and how easy it is in comparison to other fasting methods. Please don't just jump into the fast. Immediately starting a fast without preparing your body can give you some dramatic hormone changes and mood changes. It can feel uncomfortable for the first couple of weeks before you start to feel better than before. So, to reduce that discomfort, it's important to have a fasting plan and follow it. A fasting plan will include things like your goals, the times you're going to eat, what you're going to eat, and what signs might make you take a break from a fast. It's also where you can write down notes about how you're doing while fasting and areas where you can improve. A fasting plan will also help you restart your fast if you end up not fasting for a couple of weeks or months. The plan is a good reminder of how far you've come and what you can do to help you feel good on the fast. So, create a fasting plan. A lot of people like to keep this as a written journal, but you can also keep your notes in an app, on a spreadsheet, or on your blog! Just make sure you have your plan and update it regularly. Once you have your notebook ready, here are our steps to transition into your fast.

Step 1: Making a Goal

In your journal, write down your goals for fasting. Why do you want to follow the 16/8 method of fasting? Is it to be healthier, to manage medical issues, or just to feel better about your daily life? Have a specific reason for doing the 16/8 method. Having a goal can help keep you motivated to continue fasting, even during difficult times.

Your goal should be a SMART goal. SMART goals are goals that are specific, measurable, achievable, relevant, and time bound.

Specific. While you might say that your goal is to get healthier in general, this isn't a specific goal. A specific goal is clear and explains exactly where you want to see improvement. Do you want to have better blood sugar levels? Do you want to lose weight or inches from your waistline? Do you want to have more focus during your day? There are a variety of possible specific goals that you can choose from to start your fast.

Measurable. Your goal, whatever it is, should be measurable. There should be measurement that helps you see that you've made improvement. Numbers are a great way to measure your goal's success, but it can also be something beyond numbers, like having a consistent mood. So long as you are tracking your goal and measuring it in some way, your goal will be measurable. If your goal is to have better blood sugar levels, then have a specific number you're aiming for every day. This number can be found by talking with your doctor. If your goal is to lose weight or inches, then have a specific number that you're looking for on the scale or on the measuring tape. If your goal is to have more focus during the day, then track that feeling every day. Many people use mood trackers to help gauge their feelings every day. Trackers like this are perfect for non-tangible goals like feeling more focused, being happier, sleeping better, etc. When you can track your goals, then it is something measurable. If you aren't meeting your goals, you'll see that in your tracking, and you'll know that you need to adjust. And if you are meeting your goals, you can celebrate each milestone and each moment you're closer to fully achieving your goal.

Achievable. Achievable goals are ones that you can reach. If your goal is to lose hundreds of pounds through fasting, that's not quite achievable or realistic. A better goal would be saying you want to lose ten pounds. This is an achievable goal. Once you meet this goal, feel free to create another one where you want to lose another ten pounds. Achievable goals should not be ones that are monumental or ones that are very idealistic. Choose goals that are realistic. We've talked before about how choosing a large goal is not likely to succeed. This is because large goals are often more like a vision far away rather than something that is smaller and doable. Having a large goal can cause your motivation to wane, which is often why people fail at New Year's resolutions. So, choose goals that are achievable. They don't have to be easy; they just must be possible.

Relevant. Let's say that you and your best friend B decide to do the 16/8 method together. This is honestly great because you'll have someone, you're accountable to and someone who supports you. But your goals for the fast should not be the same. Your goals need to be relevant to you. Hugh Jackman did the 16/8 method for preparing his Wolverine role. Does this mean that you should follow his same goals of muscle growth and weight loss? No. He had trainers, nutritionists, and coaches that helped him reach those goals. You probably don't have that support. Besides, are you trying to look like Wolverine? Probably not. Choose goals that are relevant to you personally. Choose the measurements that work for you. Friend B might want to lose 20 pounds, but you might want to just sleep better. So long as the goal is yours, it will be relevant.

Time-bound. Goals that have a specific time to be achieved are beneficial. This doesn't mean that once you've reached your goal, you stop. You can stop if you want to, but you can also repeat the same goal again or make another goal to follow. If your goal is to have better blood sugar levels, when do you want this to happen? If you want to lose weight, when will you achieve this goal? If you want to have more focus at work, at what point will you say you've achieved your goals?

Now that you know what SMART goals are, let's look at a couple of examples of SMART goals. We'll use the examples mentioned above of losing weight, getting better blood sugar levels, and having more focus at work. Here's what a SMART goal might look like:

"I want to lose ten pounds in the next two months through fasting and cooking at home more. I want to fit into my jeans, so I will measure my success by the numbers on the scale and how easily I can slide my jeans over my belly."

This goal is specific because it's clear the person wants to lose weight to fit into their jeans. It's measurable because it has a clear number of ten pounds that can be weighed on a scale. It's achievable because most people can lose ten pounds in two months with changes to their eating schedule and their food. It's also relevant because it's a very personal goal: to fit into their jeans again. Goals don't have to be relevant to anyone else. Just make sure they're relevant to you. Finally, this goal is time-bound, with a deadline of two months. So, this goal is a better-written goal than just saying, "I want to lose weight."

"I want my blood sugar levels after waking up to go down from 150 to 90 points. I want these points to be consistent over the course of two weeks, and

I'll achieve this goal in two months by focusing on fasting, my eating habits, and walking 30 minutes every day."

This goal is specific. The person knows exactly what numbers they want to achieve. They probably tested their blood sugar for two weeks after waking up and realized that it was around 150 most or every day. This isn't a healthy blood sugar level after not eating for eight hours. So, they know they want to drop it into a healthy range that is less than 100. The goal is also measurable. We have clear numbers that they can check with a glucose monitor. Having two months to meet this goal makes it achievable, especially through fasting, better eating habits, and exercise. In fact, they may achieve their goal in less time! This goal is relevant to this person because it has specific numbers that they've learned from their own testing. Finally, this goal is time-bound because they have two months to complete it. They also know that the number 90 must be reached for multiple days before they consider the goal to have been met.

"Donna told me that I'm always spacey at work, and I always feel so tired. I want to feel more focused at work by having a less foggy mind and better concentration to work hard. I'll achieve this goal within two months through fasting and having a consistent sleep schedule. I'll also need to feel focused for five consecutive days for me to achieve the goal."

This goal is different from the previous goals because it is something that is intangible. There are no numbers to check. So, this person can measure their goals through a mood tracker that they use every day, or they can keep daily notes in their journal. They may even choose to measure the success of their work projects being completed as a sign of having more focus. Whichever way they choose to measure it, they should write it down as a part of their goal. This goal is achievable and relevant. It gives a very large time frame and fasting with eight hours of sleep can definitely help a person to feel less spacey. Because this person has feedback from others and feels foggy herself, she has a very relevant goal. This goal is also time-bound because this person set two months to achieve more focus, and there is a goal of feeling focused for five consecutive days before the goal is met. So, this goal is a decent SMART goal. All they must do is choose their measurement method for this intangible goal.

By having your goals written down in your journal and having SMART goals, you'll be able to see if intermittent fasting is helping you. You'll also be able to find areas where your goals need to be improved. The journal will help you keep your motivation up.

Step 2: Planning Your Eating Schedule (and Your Sleeping Schedule!)

This is a critical step. You can plan what to eat and where to eat it, but with the 16/8 method, it's all about when you eat. Remember, you only have an eight-hour window to eat, so what time will you have breakfast (or will you not have breakfast), what time will you have lunch, and when will you have dinner? Consider things like your current work schedule or family schedule. Do you want to eat dinner right before the beginning of your fasting time, or do you want to eat it a bit earlier? Consider all these factors. If you exercise regularly, you'll want to eat immediately after eating. However, this is just a suggestion. Some people feel weak if they don't eat something before exercising, so choose your schedule based on your feeling. Also, consider special events. How will your schedule change have based on these events? At the end of this chapter, we'll share some example fasting schedules, but be sure to adapt them to your own life.

One thing to consider when making your schedule is following your natural circadian rhythm. We've discussed this in chapter 1, but this is a recommended schedule. It sometimes doesn't work for many people. During your day, your metabolism is often fastest in the morning and slumps around 3:00 p.m. At this point, it begins its slow-down process preparing for the night. So, you can choose to have your eating window from 7:00 a.m. to 3:00 p.m. and eat you meals there, following your circadian rhythm. However, remember that this schedule doesn't work for everyone. It also doesn't give you the opportunity to eat during social events in the evening. While it doesn't give you a social life mealtime, you can always adjust your fasting and eating window to fit a planned event. You don't want to be the only one at the table who is drinking a glass of water while everyone else eats. So, plan when you'll eat to fit your own lifestyle.

It's ideal to follow the 16/8 method daily, and most people do. However, you don't have to! Some people follow it during the workweek but then skip the weekends to better fit in social eating and drinking.

Choose whatever will work for you. You can also work with your doctor to help plan out your schedule. While we're talking about schedules, it's important to also have a consistent sleep schedule. Set a consistent time to go to bed and a consistent time to wake up and follow it. This will help you figure out how many hours you need to fast each day. If you're going to go to bed at 11:00 p.m. and wake up at 7:a.m., then you can fit your fasting schedule around that. You could do your additional eight hours of fasting before you go to bed, or you could divide it into four hours before bed and four hours after you wake up. If you have a consistent sleep time but don't follow it, then it's useless. So, make sure you're following it. If you know it takes you 30 minutes of downtime before you fall asleep, then be in bed 30 minutes earlier, read a book, have some water, and then try to fall asleep at your set time. Use your alarm clock to wake up and don't keep hitting the snooze button. Overall, this consistency will help you better manage your fast.

Step 3: Planning Your Meals

Here comes the science. You need to find meals that will fit in your daily nutrition requirements and calories and keep you full. Consider snacks. Will you snack during your day? How will you break your fast? With a full meal, protein drink, or nothing? All of this should take into consideration your daily activities. If you're exercising, you'll want to make sure you have enough energy to both exercise and not be hungry during the fasting period. You can experiment with meals and then write down the results of those meals in your fasting journal. Did you feel hungry quickly after eating? Then you'll need to change around your meal. If you find that you're craving something, then you might be missing a nutrient in your meal. For example, if you're craving peanut butter, add more protein to your meals. In general, the health department has some good guidelines for how many calories to eat per day. You can then divide these calories into your meals and your snacks (if you choose to snack). All this information below is from health.gov. Because these values are for an "average" adult in height and weight, you'll need to calculate it further based on your own weight and height. You can use various websites to find the right calories for maintaining or losing weight.

Here are your recommended daily calories if you are sedentary, of average height, and average weight provided by health.gov:

AGE	Female (5'4", 126lbs.)
19 – 25	2000
26 – 50	1800
>46	1600

AGE	Male (5'10", 154 lbs.)
19 – 20	2600
21 – 40	2400
41 – 60	2200
>61	2000

Here are your recommended daily calories if you're moderately active, of average height, and average weight:

AGE	Female (5'4", 126lbs.)
19 – 25	2200
26 – 50	2000
>46	1800

AGE	Male (5'10", 154 lbs.)
19 – 25	2800
26 – 45	2600
46 – 65	2400
>66	2300

While these are suggested calories, remember that with intermittent fasting and the 16/8 method, many people end up having unplanned calorie restriction. Much of this is anecdotal, but many people have a hard time eating this many calorie in eight hours. Try to ensure you're getting enough calories in a day with enough nutrition. But if you end up taking in a couple of hundred fewer calories because you simply can't eat that much, that's okay.

Now, you don't have to count calories for this fast. A lot of people like to so that they know their meals will keep them full, but it's not a requirement. So long as you are choosing well-balanced meals that are both plentiful and nutritious, you'll be okay. Don't eat junk for an entire meal because then you'll just be hungry an hour later.

We'll explore more about possible foods and menus for your 16/8 fast in a later chapter.

Step 4: Taking a Before Picture

This isn't really a requirement, but many people find it incredibly motivating. Not only can it motivate you, but your before picture can motivate others too. If you look at a variety of blogs about people's journeys with fasting, you'll always see a before and after/current picture. This can be really motivating for the person in the picture to see their change. Seeing the physical differences in your body from before and after your fast can make you feel happy. So, take a before picture! Add it to your journal, and as you reach some of your goals, take other pictures to commemorate your success.

Step 5: Sleeping Well the Night before You Start

Now we're getting into starting the fast. The day before you start your new fast, you want to make sure you begin your preparation. Try to sleep well before you start. This will help your body prepare itself and start the process of syncing your circadian rhythm. Remember, it's a process, and you want to start on the right foot. The next day (day 1 of your fast), have a good breakfast. That night, you'll start your fasting hours.

Step 6: Starting the Transition

Start your fast gradually. Don't start by doing all 16 hours at once. Instead, break it down over the course of a couple of weeks. Assuming you sleep for eight hours a night, you only need to fast an additional eight hours during your waking hours. In week 1, for the first three days, stop eating an hour before you go to bed, and start eating one hour after you wake up. This puts you at a 10-hour fast, with 14 hours to eat. After those first three days, you're going to add an hour to before bed and after waking up. So, you'll stop eating two hours before bed and start eating two hours after waking up. This puts you at a 12hour fast, with 12 hours to eat. Three days later, add another two hours, bringing you up to a 14-hour fast, and a 10-hour eating period. Then finally, extend to the full 16 hours of fasting and 8 hours of eating. This should slowly get you into the full fast and help curb the discomfort you might feel. This will take about two weeks to get to the full fast.

One thing to mention is that exercise should be reduced during this time, and water consumption should be increased. As you get used to the fast, you can increase your exercise, but just at the beginning, you might struggle with exercising with fasting. You should also be drinking a lot more liquid as you transition into the fast. You'll want to keep hydrated because your body will start noticing that there is a larger and larger window of nothing coming in. Have water to keep you hydrated and help curb your appetite if you're feeling hungry during your fasting window.

You are, of course, welcome to just jump in and do the full 16 hours of fasting and 8 hours of eating, but with this jump into fasting, you'll have some discomfort for the first week or so. We'll discuss discomfort in the next step.

Step 7: Preparing Yourself for Magic . . . and Discomfort

While starting your fast, you need to prepare yourself for some changes to your body and habits. You might feel some discomfort with the change. This includes things like strange sleep patterns or dreams, changes in your mood, and sometimes bloating or digestive discomfort. These will usually pass after a couple of weeks of fasting. Some people are lucky and never feel the discomfort, but others do. Take the time to evaluate what you're feeling. If something is feeling way off, stop fasting and talk to your doctor. Signs to stop and talk with your doctor are feelings of weakness and dizziness, changes to your heart rate or respiration, and severe discomfort. It's very likely that you'll also feel some positive changes within the first week. Many people feel like their brains are clearer. This means that they have more focus and awareness of their environment, with less fogginess. This is a great feeling. It comes with the changes to your hormonal patterns but also the reset to your circadian rhythm. Embrace the change! Within a couple of weeks, you'll notice other changes. In research, after eight weeks of fasting, there were decent metabolic changes that people were able to maintain. This includes changes to blood glucose levels, insulin levels, and other hormones. These changes will make you feel better than you're used to, which is a great benefit that comes with fasting.

Step 8: Recording Your Progress

The final step is to keep track of your progress and record it all in your fasting journal. Note times when your meals didn't work out and times when they did. Also, record times when you felt discomfort and times when you felt fantastic with your fast! Include pictures, little motivational notes— really, anything that will help you keep on track.

Check your journal regularly. This can give you some motivation, but it can also help you find areas to tweak your fast to better fit your life. Your journal is your journey recorded. You can use it to help motivate others but also remind you of the progress you have made. Keep it up and keep recording your progress.

Starting from Previous Fast: Transitioning from the Different Types

If you're transitioning from a different type of fasting to 16/8 method, then you might find that it's less restrictive than other types of fasting. There are so many different types of fasts, so the steps for change are going to be presented here in general. If you have already made your clear SMART goals with your previous fast and that you know what you can eat for each meal, then you're ready to begin the transition into the 16/8 method. One thing with the 16/8 method is that it is eating your full calories in one day, so there isn't any calorie restriction unless you want to do that. This is very different from that of other fast types. So, ensure that you are taking enough calories to be okay during your new fasting window.

Step 1: Planning Your Eating Schedule

This may be the biggest change that you experience as you transition from other fasting types. If you were previously doing the 14/10 method, then this won't be a huge change, but if you're transitioning from the 5:2 method or the alternate-day method, then you'll need to work on your eating schedule. You only have eight hours to eat during your day, so you need to plan when you'll have your meals. This will help ensure you don't get hangry during your day and you have enough in your system to keep you good during your fast time. Determine how you are going to break your fast and end your fast. Consider when you'll eat during the day and how that will fit into your regular schedule. Also consider how you'll handle special occasions with your friends and family.

Just like it was discussed in the transition for beginners, consider whether you will follow this fast daily or only a couple days a week. You'll reap the most benefits from a daily fast, but it's up to you and your lifestyle.

One thing to consider when making your schedule is following your natural circadian rhythm. This was discussed in detail in chapter 1 and again in the section about transitioning from scratch, but we're mentioning it again in case you skipped that section. Following your circadian rhythm is something to keep in mind for your fasting schedule. Most people have a slump in the middle of the day, around 3:00 p.m. You have the most energy in the morning, so you want to take advantage of your natural circadian rhythm. Then you can time you're eating window to start at 7:00 a.m. and end at 3:00 p.m. This will put your body in a better metabolic state and help your body burn more fat than if you eat late at night. This schedule might not work for everyone, especially if you do shift work or if you have a family you're caring for. So, find a schedule that works for you and take advantage of the times you feel naturally more energized in your day.

Finally, ensure that you are also maintaining your own sleep schedule. You'll need to have a set sleeping time and waking time to better time your fast. If you followed the 5:2 method or alternate-day method, this might not have been so important.

After all, you could eat regularly every other day, and it didn't really matter how many hours you slept. However, having a set sleep schedule will help you determine how many hours to fast while on the 16/8 method. If you sleep eight hours a night, you will only need to fast for an additional eight hours when you're awake. If you get less sleep, you'll need to adjust your fasting time during the day.

Step 2: Starting Your Transition

Your transition schedule is going to follow the same as the beginner's schedule, except you'll need to start from a day when you've done regular eating. If you're currently following the 5:2 method or the alternate-day method, make sure that you are eating enough calories the day before you start your new fast schedule. Then that night, you can start your fast. Here's the schedule, which is the same for beginners:

In week 1, for the first three days, stop eating an hour before you go to bed and start eating one hour after you wake up. This puts you at a 10-hour fast, with 14 hours to eat. After those first three days, you're going to add an hour before bed and after waking up. So, you'll stop eating two hours before bed and start eating two hours after waking up. This puts you at 12 hours of fasting and 12 hours of eating. Three days later, add another two hours, bringing you up to 14 hours of fasting and 10 hours of eating. Then finally, extend to the full 16 hours of fasting and 8 hours of eating. This schedule is perfect if you're planning on doing the midday eating window or late day eating window. But if you want to do an early morning eating window, then move your fasting hours to before bed. For instance, in the first three days, stop eating two hours before bed. Then the next three days, stop eating four hours before bed. Continue until the last three transition days, where you stop eating six or eight hours before bed.

Both transitions should slowly get you into the full fast and help curb the discomfort you might feel. This will take about two weeks to get to the full fast. You can jump right into the 16/8 method if you were previously following the 12/12 method or the 14/10 method. You can jump right into the 16/8 from any other method, too, but you might experience some discomfort from the change.

Step 3: Preparing for Discomfort

Since you've fasted before, you probably know about the discomfort you might feel at the beginning of a new fast. If you're transitioning from a fast that included severe calorie restrictions, like the 5:2 fast, then be prepared for how eating more in a day will change your body. You might feel bloated or some gastric distress. For everyone else who has been fasting without calorie restrictions, just keep in mind that each transition brings its own level of discomfort. You might not have any issues if you're changing from the 14/10 fast to the 16/8 fast, but just be prepared in case. Keep in mind any warning signs that you should talk to a doctor about. Things like dizziness, vertigo, feeling weak, or changes in your heart rate all require you to see your doctor. If you're feeling particularly weak after shifting to the 16/8 method, then make sure that your meals have enough calories and are well-balanced.

Step 4: Recording Things in Your Journal

Keep a fasting journal for your 16/8 fast. If you've kept one before, then just add to it with your new fasting plan. Record your new goals, all the changes you're going through, and what you are experiencing with the change in eating schedule. Find areas where you are feeling better with the change and areas where you might be feeling discomfort. It's important to record these instances because you can then go back and determine what might be causing discomfort. Maybe it was a meal you ate or poor sleep the night before. Having a record of your day to day while fasting can help you control how your body is feeling. One thing to record is your meals. You want to make sure you're getting enough calories during the day and that you're feeling full enough that you won't be hungry in the middle of the day.

Typical Schedule for the 16/8 method

We've gone over the step-by-step process of transitioning into your fast. We've also looked a bit at making sure you have a clear record of the steps you are taking and how your body is adapting to the fast. Now let's look at some possible schedules for your fast. There is a schedule for your transition period and a schedule that examines what your daily eating times and windows will look like. Here are some additional things to keep in mind before looking at schedules:

• Your choice of schedule is personal. Create one based on your work schedule or other circumstances in your life. If you want to have dinner with your family, then use that meal to close out your eating window. Count back eight hours to figure out when your first meal will be.

• Your fasting schedule doesn't have to be set in stone. Try out different times or change your fasting window for special occasions. You don't want to be limited by your schedule, especially when it comes to your social life.

• A great option for scheduling is to follow the times when you're naturally more awake and aware and end your fast before your natural slumps. Each person has a different internal clock, so determine your schedule based on that. Following your natural circadian rhythm is a good place to start; adapt from there.

Early Eating Schedule

This schedule is a great option because it takes advantage of your circadian rhythm. It also is the ideal time in general to eat because it avoids eating late at night. However, it means that you're going to eat an early dinner, which might not work for everyone. With this schedule, you'll start eating at 7:00 a.m. and end at 3:00 p.m.

Here is how to ease into your fast:

TIME	DAY 1-3	DAY 4-6	DAY 7-9	DAY 10-12
7 AM	WAKE UP	WAKE UP	WAKE UP	WAKE UP
9 AM	EAT	EAT	EAT	EAT
11 AM	FAST	FAST	FAST	FAST
1 PM	EAT	EAT	EAT	EAT
5 PM	SNACK	EAT	EAT	EAT BEFORE 3PM
7 PM	EAT	EAT	FAST	FAST
9 PM	EAT	FAST	FAST	FAST
10 PM	FAST	FAST	FAST	FAST
11 PM	SLEEP/FAST	SLEEP/FAST	SLEEP/FAST	SLEEP/FAST

Here is your weeklong schedule once you've eased into the fast:

TIME	FROM MONDAY TO SUNDAY
12 AM – 7 AM	SLEEP/FAST
7 AM – 2 PM	BREAKFAST/LARGEST MEAL OF THE DAY
2 PM – 3 PM	LAST MEAL OF THE DAY
3 PM - 12 AM	SLEEP/FAST

Midday Eating Schedule

Some people have difficulty with eating first thing in the morning. In this case, you can start your fast later in the day. This fast is ideal for people who want to eat right in the middle of the day. It gives you time to wind down before bed and prepare your body for a time of rest without too much digestion happening while you sleep. It also gives you time to exercise in the morning before you break your fast if you want to.

Evening Eating Schedule

This schedule doesn't take advantage of your circadian rhythm, and it might not give you the most benefits in changing glucose and cortisol levels. However, this schedule can work for people who really appreciate social eating or people who work at unconventional hours. You can always eat a bit earlier to change this schedule.

Here is how to ease into your fast:

TIME	DAY 1-3	DAY 4-6	DAY 7-9	DAY 10-12
12 AM	SLEEP/FAST	SLEEP/FAST	SLEEP/FAST	SLEEP/FAST
6 AM	FAST	FAST	FAST	FAST
8 AM	FAST	FAST	FAST	FAST
10 AM	EAT	FAST	FAST	FAST
12 PM	EAT	EAT	FAST	FAST
2 PM	EAT	EAT	FAST	FAST
4 PM	SNACK	EAT	SNACK	EAT
6 PM	SNACK	EAT	EAT	EAT
8 PM	EAT	EAT	EAT	EAT
10 PM	EAT	EAT	EAT	EAT
12 PM	EAT	EAT	EAT	EAT BEFORE MIDNIGHT

Here is your week-long schedule once you've eased into the fast:

TIME	FROM MONDAY TO SUNDAY
12 AM – 8 AM	SLEEP/FAST
8 AM – 4 PM	FAST
4 PM – 8 PM	BREAKFAST/LARGEST MEAL OF THE DAY
11 PM - 12 AM	LARGE MEAL (LAST MEAL FINISHED BY MIDNIGHT)

These three different schedules give you some options for following your 16/8 fasting schedule. As mentioned before, adapt the schedules to better fit your own daily rhythm and lifestyle. It's ideal if your schedule is consistent, but it doesn't have to be set in stone. If you know you want to celebrate your best friend's promotion at the end of the week, then shift your fasting schedule to accommodate eating with your friends. Remember, fasting isn't a diet; it's just an eating schedule. It doesn't need to be permanent, and there shouldn't be any guilt about shifting your schedule. Since we've now discussed several schedule possibilities and how to ease into them, we'll spend the next couple of chapters looking at food choices and some meal plans.

Chapter 10
Combining Specific Diets and Intermittent Fasting

We've discussed when to eat. Now let's start exploring what to eat. As we start looking into what we eat, it's important to discuss the possibility of "supercharging" your fast by adding a diet. Before we get into the different types of diets you can combine with the 16/8 method of intermittent fasting, it's important to make sure you understand the goals. We'll also discuss the benefits and risks and when to combine the two. Before you consider adding a diet to your fast, please make sure you talk to a doctor, especially if you have a medical condition you're concerned about.

Intermittent fasting isn't a diet. It doesn't require any changes to the type of food you eat, though that's recommended if you want to reap the most benefits. While most people will simply eat well-balanced, nutritious meals, you may want to add a diet if you have a very specific goal. If you are already dieting and you want to add intermittent fasting to your eating plan, then that's great! Just keep in mind that fasting will add some additional stress to your body, and it won't be compatible with some diets. Some example diets that don't work with intermittent fasting are very-low-calorie diets, diets that only focus on one or two food items, and any diet that is marketed as a cleanse.

Very low-calorie diets (like 800 calories a day) and fasting don't mix for some pretty obvious reasons. If you're not getting enough calories and you're not eating frequently, then you've created a dangerous recipe. Your body won't do well with such a restriction, and it's likely that you'll be malnourished and go into "starvation mode," where your body starts slowing down your metabolism. So, you won't see any results with this type of diet.

Diets that focus only on one food item or group will also backfire with a fasting diet. Fasting requires you to have enough energy from your food to make sure you're functioning well during your day, but if your food choice is only, say, cabbage soup, you're not going to get the right nutrients to power your day. You'll end up feeling weak, faint, or nauseous. It's also likely that remaining on such a diet will cause you to have some malnourishment, as there is no way you're getting enough nutrition from cabbage soup alone.

Finally, diets that claim to be "cleansing" diets won't really work with fasting. This is because most cleansing diets are liquid-based and don't really offer nutrition. You will feel incredibly hungry on these cleanses while also fasting. Cleanses aren't necessary since your body can handle itself. So instead, choose diets that are nutritious, healthy, and will provide your body with enough energy to get through your fasting period.

There are two diets that do work well with intermittent fasting and have some scientific research to back it up. These two diets are the keto diet and some basic calorie restriction. Some people do more calorie restriction than the unplanned version that naturally comes with fasting but still eat more than 1,200 calories a day. Whichever way you choose, please proceed with caution. You don't want to end up in a state where you are shaking and have a foggy mind. Let's look at these two types of diets.

Keto

The keto diet can help people lose weight, but did you also know that it has been historically used to reduce epilepsy? The keto diet can also help with several diseases like diabetes, skin issues, heart disease, and cancer (Paoli et al., 2013). There is a lot of research to back up these claims. While most people today use the diet to lose weight, it's also a great option for people who are struggling with a variety of diseases. It uses food as medicine to help heal your body. For people who have epilepsy, eating very low-carb foods every day can help ease symptoms and even replace medications. Of course, please just don't throw your meds out. Talk to your doctor first.

So, the keto diet has a lot of positives, but why does it work? In the keto diet, you reduce your carbohydrates and increase your healthy fats and proteins. Your carbs are greatly reduced. It's not just a low-carb diet but a very-low-carb diet. Instead of eating carbs, you're eating more healthy fats. The whole purpose of the keto diet is to put your body in a state of ketosis. In this state, your body starts burning a lot of your stored fat instead of taking energy from carbs (that you're no longer eating). This may sound familiar since intermittent fasting does a very similar thing. It also puts your body into a state of using your stores of fat during the fasting period rather than using what you recently ate. Therefore, the keto diet and intermittent fasting can work together so well.

Ketosis is a state where the body uses fat for energy. The body uses ketones to fuel itself instead of relying on glucose, which is what we get out of carbs and sugary foods. The science behind ketosis and reaching that state is beyond this book's purpose. So, to get to the point, to follow the keto diet, you need to reach the stage of ketosis. To reach this metabolic state, you must consume less than 50 grams of carbohydrates a day. That is not a lot at all. This is about 5% of your daily nutrition in comparison to our normal carb intake, which is well over 50% of our daily nutrition. So, it can be a little difficult to start the process of reducing carbs in such a drastic way.

Ketosis shouldn't be confused with ketoacidosis. Ketosis is healthy. Ketoacidosis is not. Ketoacidosis can affect someone with uncontrollable diabetes or uncontrollable alcohol consumption. It is the result of very high blood sugar levels that then turn your normal, benign blood into something that is highly acidic. Acid running through your veins is not healthy. If left untreated, ketoacidosis is deadly.

So, the keto diet's purpose is to get you into the state of ketosis. It's in this state that you'll burn your fat stores and lose weight. You'll also reap the other benefits of ketosis. Because you are losing your fat stores, you don't have to count your calories. You'll still eat large portions, just without the carbs. The absence of carbs means that you won't be converting it into stores of fat for later energy. You'll be replacing the carbs with higher amounts of healthy fats and proteins. This means you'll feel fuller longer and eating this way will suppress some of your appetite and cravings.

Combining fasting with the keto diet can help you shed more weight and reach ketosis faster than doing the keto diet alone. This is because fasting already primes your body to burn more fat instead of requiring carbs for an energy source. This is something closely connected to the keto diet.

Calorie Restriction

Calorie restriction is your typical diet. It's what most doctors and nutritionists recommend helping you lose weight. With calorie restriction, you are greatly reducing the number of calories you are eating each day. This results in weight loss because you simply are not eating as much as you used to.

To determine how many calories to reduce, you can use a calorie calculator online. You'll input information like your age, sex, height, and current weight. The calculator will give you information for the calories you need to eat to maintain your current weight and calories to eat to lose weight. All this calculation is just the beginning, though. You must do something with the information.

To do calorie restriction, you'll have to count your calories for every food item you eat. You can do this with apps that can calculate your calories based on food items. This is helpful for items that didn't come in a package. There isn't a "required" food to eat, but generally, you want to have a wellbalanced diet when doing calorie restriction. This is because if you don't, your body may interpret your diet as starvation. The results of this will be some severe physiological responses.

The 16/8 method of intermittent fasting can result in unplanned calorie restriction, but you can up it a bit by doing it on purpose. Start by calculating the calories you need to eat to lose weight while also not being malnourished, and then plan your meals accordingly. Remember to keep your meals well balanced and record all the calories you eat.

Benefits and Risks

So, combining the keto and intermittent fasting could lead to better glucose levels, lower insulin levels, and better weight loss. Combining calorie restriction with intermittent fasting can result in weight loss, better physiological health, and better aging.

The risks associated with combining intermittent fasting and the keto diet or calorie restriction and the 16/8 method are like the risks already mentioned in chapter one. It's important to talk to your doctor or nutritionist before combining the fast with a diet. This will help you plan the appropriate steps and better understand the risks associated with combining.

Some people may find it difficult to start and maintain the keto diet. Since it's a restrictive diet, a lot of people's favorite foods may not fit into the diet. This can cause some people to struggle. A way to go about reducing this discomfort is to make the change slowly. Just like we do for intermittent fasting, take a couple of weeks to make your changes so that it's not such a jarring huge change. This may make it easier to follow the keto diet.

When first starting keto, a lot of people feel some physiological changes that aren't positive. This includes poor sleep, a feeling of fogginess, and digestive issues. It can also cause some difficulty with your energy levels, and this includes when you exercise. You'll need to be prepared for any of these feelings, and they'll pass after a couple of weeks while following keto.

There is an additional risk that you may lose some muscle when dieting with keto or doing calorie restriction. This is a risk that comes with any diet. Your body will start taking energy from your muscles instead of your fats if you're not getting enough protein or nutrients. To reduce this risk, make sure that you are eating enough and that it is well-balanced food. Don't just eat junk and expect your body to be okay with it. You'll lose more muscle like that.

With calorie restriction, there are risks like restricting your calories too much. If you do this while on a fast, your body will go into starvation mode, and you won't lose any weight. In fact, each time you eat, your body will start storing energy to prepare for the "starvation" period. Another risk is that you won't eat enough high-quality meals. This can lead to hunger during your fasting window. This isn't ideal, obviously. So, to combat this, make sure you eat well-balanced meals as part of your calorie restriction. It's important to get enough nutrition, so don't base all your food around one food group only. When to Combine Them

If you're interested in following a specific diet while following your 16/8 fast, then there are a couple of ways you can combine them. First off, it's not recommended to start them both at the same time. Do you remember how we discussed making big goals and how they fail? Combining intermittent fasting with a diet right off the bat is a huge goal. Not only are you changing when you eat, but now you're also changing what you eat at the same time. That's a lot of change. It will cause your body a lot of stress, especially as you keep extending your fasting window. Instead, it's better to start either you diet first or your fast. Then later, you add the second part. If you're going to start your diet first, follow your normal eating schedule. Change what you eat to fit your diet's requirements. If you're following the keto diet, this is a good way to start changing your metabolic state, which will also be enhanced by fasting at a later point. Remember that with the keto diet, you're going to have several weeks of discomfort as your body shifts into ketosis. This discomfort will pass eventually, so don't be alarmed. You'll notice things like changes in bowel movements, having different energy levels, and having mood swings. These symptoms won't pass very quickly, so take your time easing into the diet and getting past the symptoms.

Once you're well situated in the keto diet and you've been symptom-free for a while, you can start adding fasting to your diet. Again, ease into the fast and be prepared for your body's reaction to this change. If you are following the keto diet on your doctor's orders, please make sure you talk to them before adding the fasting component. You don't want to make too many changes to your metabolic levels without your doctor knowing if they gave you the green light for keto. If you're going at it alone and are already relatively healthy, then combine the two diets, and if you feel any severe discomfort, talk to your doctor.

If you're going to start with caloric restriction first, then again follow your normal eating times. Make sure that you are well versed in how many calories you can eat per day and what foods help you meet those goals. As you change your calorie intake, you may feel hungry more often and may experience feelings like fatigue and weakness. If the discomfort becomes severe, talk to your doctor. Once you've been following your calorie changes for a while and once you've reached a point where it feels comfortable, you can combine it with your fast. Here, you want to make sure that your fast doesn't result in further calorie restrictions. So, you want to be very consistent with what you're eating and make sure you are always counting calories. Your daily calorie limit should not change once you start your fast because you're already at a reduced calorie limit. If it does change, you're at risk for malnourishment and other side effects from the fast itself. It is very important that you keep a record of your calorie intake while you fast if you are following a calorie restricted diet.

If you decide to try fasting before adding on diets, make sure you are taking the time to ease into the fast. You also want to make sure you're eating those well-balanced meals we keep talking about. This will help you transition easier into the fast. Once you've been following the 16/8 fast for a while, try incorporating your diet of choice. If you want to follow the keto diet, then make sure that you are cutting down on the carbs. This will push your body into ketosis. You may feel a lot of discomfort with this change, as your body will need to adapt to the new eating pattern you're following. If you decide to try calorie restriction, start by calculating how many calories you're currently eating in a day while fasting. Do this for a week. There's a chance that you're already eating fewer calories and already at your calorie goal for weight loss. So, it's important to check first. If you still need to cut calories, then do so carefully. You want to make sure that you still have enough food to keep you energized through your fast.

Throughout this entire process, keep journaling about your progress. This will help you keep on track, but also it will help you find areas that need improvement. Journaling is also a great way to keep track of foods, diets, or eating times that didn't work for you and why. This way, you won't do the same thing again. Now that we've talked about combining diets with the 16/8 method, let's look at what to eat while intermittent fasting.

Chapter 11
Sample Menus for Intermittent Fasting

Now we're getting to the nitty-gritty of your intermittent fast. This chapter is all about what to eat, with some specific suggestions. There's no possible way to cover every type of meal you can eat while you're fasting, so follow some of our suggestions, and then find some recipes that work for you. Make sure they also follow your diet of choice, or just eat well-balanced meals. Remember, you don't have to change your diet at all. If you're already eating healthy foods, then great! Keep doing it while you're fasting. But if you're like most of the people in the United States and fast food is a major food group, then consider changing to eating well-balanced, homecooked meals. If you choose to continue eating as is, with large servings of fast food during the week, that's your choice. However, don't expect to see as many positive results as you would if you were eating a well-balanced meal. Also, if you are currently on the cabbage soup diet or gummy worm diet, then we highly recommend you start eating well-balanced meals. Please.

One thing to mention is that as you fast, you can drink liquids like water, black coffee, and unsweetened tea. You should drink a lot of water. Maybe even more than you would if you weren't fasting. We get a lot of hydration from the foods we eat, but if we're only eating in an eight-hour window, then we'll have less hydration. So, make sure you're drinking enough water. Add a pinch of sea salt to the water to ensure you're maintaining your electrolytes too. In this chapter, we're going to look at some specifics of what you eat during your fast. We'll go over how to break your fast and what foods can help you start your day. We'll also cover some foods that can bring your eating window to a close. We'll also look at some wellbalanced meals that can help make the fasting period easier. These meals will help you get through your fasting period and can help you have better health on top of the benefits you'll get from fasting. There will also be some suggestions for foods to eat if you are choosing to follow a diet while fasting. All these sections are recommendations and don't have to be followed to the letter.

What to Eat First Thing in the Morning

When you are ready to break your fast, you're going to feel hungry. Depending on the schedule of your meals, your first "breakfast" could be at 7:00 a.m., or it could be way later at 4:00 p.m. Either way, you'll want to ensure that what you eat isn't going to cause you issues down the road. Your first meal should be something light. Even though a whole pizza or a burger might sound really tempting, please believe us that eating that first will put you into a world of pain. Eating something very heavy to break your fast can give you indigestion, a churning stomach, the runs, and can even make you feel nauseous. So please, save your heavy foods for another time.

Start with some light, easy-to-digest foods. If you're choosing to have a small mini breakfast before eating two larger meals during the day, start with some liquid. A lot of people like starting with coffee or tea, but first, start with water. You want to make sure you're getting enough hydration to start your eating window. After having some water, go ahead and have your coffee, tea, juice, etc. Bone broth is also an excellent way to start.

You could have a fruit smoothie if you want to, but make sure the fruits have a low glycemic index. This means that they won't drastically increase your blood sugar levels. This advice works for some people, especially if you're watching your blood sugar levels. You want to avoid a huge spike in your blood sugar levels because your fast has just helped to stabilize them. So, try to avoid sugar and carbs to break your fast. That means no sugar in your tea, coffee, or smoothie. Added sugar and carbs will make you feel bloated and can cause a later drop in your blood sugar levels, and that's not how you want to start your day. If you want to experiment with your body's response to sugar and carbs in your first meal, go ahead. You could start with oatmeal or granola for breakfast and add fruit or a smoothie. This will give you a good amount of fiber and some carbs and sugars too. Make sure you note your body's response to eating this in your fasting journal. This way, you can decide on what types of food are good for you to break your fast with and which ones should be avoided.

Next to the liquid, add some easily digestible proteins or vegetables. Yogurt or eggs can be a great way to start because they provide you with protein and some healthy fats. If you want to make a super healthy breakfast, try balancing a healthy fat with some protein and fiber. Just make sure you are making a note of what you're eating so that if you feel adverse effects later, you know what you can change.

If your first meal is going to be one of your larger ones, then make sure you eat until you are full.

What to Eat at the End of Your Eating Window?

As your eating window ends, you want to have a last full meal. This shouldn't be a little snack. Eat until you're full so that your body can carry over some of the energy into your fasting window. You want to have a good mix of protein, fiber, and healthy fats, just like you would for your breakfast. These nutrients will help you feel full longer. So have a wellbalanced meal for dinner and make sure you are eating enough to feel full. Now is not the time to only have half an apple for dinner.

Remember that your meals should be robust, but you shouldn't be overeating. Overeating will not help your body and will result in your fast being ineffective. You'll be likely to gain weight instead of losing it, and your blood sugar levels may not stabilize. So, once you start your eating window, eat slow and steady and don't binge just because you're hungry.

Fasting with Basic Nutritional Guidelines

If you have gone to school in the United States, then you've heard what makes a good meal. We've seen the charts, and the food pyramid, but what does that look like while on your plate? And how do we even choose the foods that will give us the best energy?

We're going to answer some of these questions in this section.

To begin with, the US government has a great website called choosemyplate.gov. On this website, you can learn about how to portion your meals so that they're well balanced. They'll even give you meal plans and how your plate should look for you. Each one is customizable based on your weight, height, sex, etc. So, if you want a more detailed look into nutritious meals and how they can work for you, check out the website. It's full of resources that can help you choose the right foods while you're fasting. When you're eating a balanced meal, you want to eat a lot of fruits and vegetables. This is your fiber. Then add some protein, healthy fats, and grains. Combining fiber and protein with every meal means that you'll feel full longer. It will satiate your hunger hormone and help you during your fasting window. Let's look at an example of what your meals could be. Half of your plate should be vegetables of fruit. About one-third of your plate should be grains, preferably whole grains or starchy vegetables. Protein like tofu, fish, meat, and beans should fill the rest of your plate, a little less than one-fourth of your plate. This is how a balanced meal looks. To add dairy, have some on the side or as a snack. It can also be a great breakfast choice. For dairy, choose fat-free or low-fat options.

Try to avoid processed foods because they have a lot of sugar and carbs that are more than you need. It's also hard to measure them as part of a wellbalanced meal. A well-balanced meal doesn't mean that you need to count calories. Instead, what you're looking at is food that will keep you full but also give you good nutrients.

Well-Balanced Breakfast Ideas

Whether your breakfast will be small or large, once you break your fast, you want to try to mix protein and fiber. Record what you eat and write down how your body feels after eating it. This will help you know what works for breaking your fast and what doesn't work. Some people react negatively to eating sugars and carbs in the morning, so keep track of your reactions to these items. Here are some breakfast ideas that give you a good mix of fiber and protein.

1.   1. Hot oatmeal with fruit, nuts, and yogurt: This is a great mix of fiber from oatmeal and fruit, healthy fats from nuts, and dairy/protein.

2.   2. Whole-grain toast and peanut butter/almond butter: Have a side of fruit to eat with it. Try one cup of blueberries or an apple. Or if you want to get crazy, slice some bananas and put them on your peanut butter toast.

3.   3. Whole-grain cereal with one cup of milk: Milk gives you your protein, and whole-grain cereal is your fiber. Some people may not find this filling enough after ending a fast. If you're still hungry, add some fruit or nuts to eat with the cereal. Make sure you read the list of ingredients on the cereal box. Some cereals claim to be "whole grain," but they're often not. Choose one that will give you good fiber content.

4.   4. Eggs and whole-grain toast: Add a side of vegetables if you want to make a larger breakfast. Think avocados for their healthy fat or try tomatoes and peppers.

5.   5. Yogurt and granola: Granola are a carb and is sugary, so proceed with some caution. Add blueberries, sliced almonds, and some flax seed for added nutrition.

6.   6. Cheese omelet with mushrooms, roasted peppers, and spinach: Eat it with a side of wholewheat toast or an English muffin.

Each of these meals combines whole-grain fiber (e.g., toast, oatmeal, granola, and cereal) with a protein (e.g., eggs, yogurt, peanut butter, milk). Follow this pattern for a breakfast that will satiate you and hold you over until the next meal. Whatever you choose to eat for breakfast, make sure that you're not binging on it. So, control your portions and eat until you are full but not overfull.

Well-Balanced Lunch Ideas

A well-balanced lunch is one that follows the "plate" discussed above. So, half of your lunch should be fruit or veggies, one-third should be grains, and slightly less than one-fourth should be protein. In this section, we'll divide up the sections of the plate and explain some options for each section. Then when you make your lunch, you can pick and choose things from each section. There's so much variety here that it's hard to just limit it to a handful of recipes. With the ingredients explained, you can choose the items that work for you and create many different meals. Try to have at least three of the food groups covered in your lunch.

7.   1. Fruit and veggies: For lunch, you could do a variety of sliced vegetables, or add them to a salad. You could even add them to a soup and get your veggies that way. For salads, try a mix of leafy greens, radishes, one-half an avocado, grape tomatoes, and carrots. Or go with one leafy green like spinach and add beets, carrots, cucumbers, and tomatoes to the salad. If salads aren't for you, experiment with sautéed vegetables like zucchini and mushrooms in soy sauce or roasted broccoli and peppers. Both options are great sides for grains and protein. If you would prefer a lunch that is more like a bunch of small sides than a full meal, choose two or three vegetables and slice them up for raw eating. When people think of food like this, they think of carrots, tomatoes, and celery. But really, any vegetable will work so long as you're okay with eating them cold.

8.   2. Grains: After you have your vegetables set up, you should add some grains. If you want a combination of grains and protein, try quinoa, barley, or buckwheat. If these are not things you're interested in, then have a side of potatoes or corn. You could even have toast or a sandwich with whole-grain bread and on the inside some meat, dairy, and vegetables. Savory oatmeal is also an option and is delicious with crumbled bacon, a poached egg, and spinach as a side.

9.   3. Protein: Your lunch proteins can be ones that are easy to eat, like sliced meats, or meatballs, which are small enough to eat without a fork or knife. However, if you want to eat a variety, try some salmon filets, a beef

stir-fry, roasted chicken breast, or tuna salad. If meat is not your thing, then try some braised tofu, roasted chickpeas, bean soup, or lentils. Eggs are also a good protein option.

10.   4. Dairy: You can add a little bit of dairy to your lunch to have more flavor. Cheese is always a welcome ingredient to most foods. You could have a glass of milk with your lunch, too, or you could have a one-half cup of yogurt to wrap up your meal. Here are some meal ideas:

•   Mason jar salad with leafy greens, vegetables, quinoa, cheese, and dressing.

•   Roasted chicken pieces and roasted potatoes, with a side of sliced peppers and tomatoes.

•   Whole roasted sweet potato with beans, cheese, salsa, and corn. A side salad can round out this lunch if the potato alone isn't enough for you.

•   Spinach and barley salad with grape tomatoes, poached eggs, feta cheese, and walnuts, plus a dressing of choice.

•   Open-faced egg salad sandwich with wholegrain toast and a side salad.

•   Bean soup, with a mix of several kinds of beans, cooked in bone broth or chicken broth. Some vegetables that work with soup are squash, celery, carrots, garlic, and onions cooked with the soup. You can also add some barley, egg noodles, or rice to the soup for your grain.

There is so much variety here. Find some recipes online that you're interested in and cook them for lunch. Just remember to include the right ratio of vegetables, fruits, grains, and proteins. The goal here is to not eat out for lunch every day. Mix it up. Choose foods, vegetables, and meats that are different so that you never get bored with your lunch. A key tip is to make your lunches on the weekend, store them in the fridge (or freezer), and then just bring them with you during your workday. Make sure that your lunch is going to keep you full and hold you over until your last meal of the day.

Well-Balanced Dinner Ideas

Dinner is obviously your last meal before your fast. If you're ending your eating window right before you go to bed, choose foods that are not going to keep you up at night. In this situation, stay away from heavily salted foods, heavy spices, or very fatty foods. These foods will disturb your sleep. If you have several hours between your last meal and bedtime, then feel free to eat things that will keep you full. Remember, the key strategy for feeling satiated is to mix protein and fiber. Meals that have these two things will keep you fuller for longer. You can repeat the ideas from the lunch area above, or you can branch out with heavier foods like stews and red meats.

<u>Here are some meal ideas:</u>

- Whole-wheat spaghetti and turkey meatballs with tomato sauce, topped with some shredded

Parmesan with a small side salad. You may add spinach to the tomato sauce.

- Salmon filet with asparagus, roasted tomatoes, and quinoa.

- Chicken curry with brown rice, spinach, and carrots.

- Bean chili with kidney, pinto, and black eye beans. Serve with whole wheat tortilla chips, cheese, and chives. The chili should have tomatoes and onions in it, but you can also add peppers, squash, or carrots to spruce it up.

- Tofu stir-fry with asparagus, bell peppers, onions, almonds, sesame seeds, and green beans. This can be served with brown rice or barley.

It's a good idea to have some variety with your dinner meals. Have some meatless meals during the week and add at least two meals with fish. This will provide you with some different nutrients and will also help so you don't get bored with your menu.

Cooking all these meals can feel really overwhelming if you're not into cooking. If you're interested, you can cook meals over the weekend and store them in the fridge or freezer. This will help ease your meal planning for the week. If you want to really try something different, you can use one of the meal deliveries services that provide you with either complete meals or the ingredients for the meals based on your nutritional requirements.

These include companies like Blue Apron, Freshly, or Plated. These can be a good option if you don't know how to cook because they'll provide everything and give you step-by-step directions on how to make their products. Either way, you want to avoid eating out every day and try to skip the easy freezer meals unless they're packages of frozen vegetables. Ramen noodles are also not a well-balanced meal despite what your roommates at college taught you.

Side Notes

Since intermittent fasting with the 16/8 method isn't a restrictive diet, you can experiment with your fast by having days when you eat out with your friends and family. Alcohol is also something you can have but only during your eating window. During your fasting period, keep your liquids to just water, black coffee, and tea. Now, a fast isn't a diet, so you don't need to have well-balanced meals. However, these will ensure that you're not hungry quickly after a meal. They'll also hold you over the 16 hours that you need to fast. In the next section, we'll talk about some food options for fasting with the keto diet.

Fasting with Keto

If you're choosing to follow the keto diet while also fasting, then there are some foods you'll want to avoid. You don't need to avoid them entirely, but you do need to reduce how much you eat. These are foods that are higher in carbs. Here is the list:

• 1. Foods with a lot of sugar and starch: This includes your typical "carbs"like bread and pasta. However, it also includes things like corn, rice, oatmeal, and barley. So, you'll need to be careful about your grain choices or eliminate them entirely. You'll also need to cut down on sugary foods, like cake, candy, white or milk chocolate, and ice cream. These foods have sugar that will spike your blood glucose levels and bring you out of ketosis.

• 2. Fruit, beans, legumes, and root vegetables: This can be surprising to a lot of people because when we think of "diet," we often think, "Eat as much fruit and vegetables as possible." However, with the keto diet, this isn't possible. Fruits, beans, legumes, and root vegetables all have higher sugars and carbs than other vegetables, so you'll need to avoid these foods. The exception to this is berries, which don't have a high number of carbs and won't spike your blood sugar levels. The root vegetables to avoid include potatoes, sweet potatoes, carrots, beets, and other starchy vegetables.

• 3. Highly processed foods: This shouldn't come as a surprise. Most diets require you to avoid highly processed foods. These types of foods tend to be heavy on sugar and carbohydrates. They also tend to have unhealthy fats in them. Speaking of which, you'll want to avoid unhealthy fats (e.g., margarine, shortening, mayonnaise, and canola oil). You'll also want to avoid foods that are labeled as diet foods or sugar-free foods. These foods are heavily processed and contain unexpected carbs and sugar alcohols that can kick you out of ketosis. The final foods to avoid include condiments that are high in carbs and sugar. That means no to ketchup and BBQ sauce.

• 4. Alcohol: Sadly, you'll have to avoid alcohol while on this diet. Beer especially is a high-carb drink. Many other alcohols have natural carbs and sugars that can spike your insulin levels, so avoid them while on your fast and keto diet.

Here are some of the foods you should incorporate into your diet. In fact, most of your meals should have these foods. While some of these foods do have carbs, they're generally low. However, make sure you're still counting your carbohydrates to make sure you're not consuming too many.

1. 1. Beef, lamb, pork, chicken, and fatty fish: All these foods have nearly zero carbs and can help you feel full longer. If you want to eat shellfish, they do have some carbs, roughly 5 grams per 100 grams of shellfish. So long as you measure it out, you'll be able to control how many carbohydrates you eat from shellfish. Fatty fish that have low to no carbs are salmon, mackerel, sardines, trout, haddock, herring, tuna, and catfish.

2. 2. Dairy like butter, eggs, cream, yogurt, and cheese: Many people are surprised by this because a lot of diets restrict how much fat you can eat. The keto diet is the opposite. So long as you are having healthy fats, you can eat them. Dairy products can provide you with healthy fats, vitamins, protein, and of course, flavor. They also keep you full for longer. Make sure that the ones you choose are unsweetened and full fat to receive the most benefits.

3. 3. Low-carb vegetables and avocados: Not all vegetables are low in carbohydrates, as we've explained briefly above. Make sure you check out

the carbs in your vegetables before buying them. In general, vegetables that are leafy greens are low in carbohydrates. Cruciferous vegetables, like broccoli and cauliflower, are also low in carbs. Tomatoes, eggplants, cucumbers, peppers, mushrooms, and onions all have less than 10 grams of carbs per 100 grams of the vegetable, so these are good vegetables to eat.

4.   4. Berries: As we mentioned above, berries are the best kinds of fruit to eat because they aren't full of carbs and sugars. Blueberries, blackberries, strawberries, and raspberries can make an excellent dessert with full-fat whipped cream.

5.   5. Nuts, seeds, and healthy oils: Some great options for omega-3s are nuts and seeds because they also count as a healthy fat. These include almonds, pistachios, pecans, and macadamia nuts. If you want to experiment with seeds, try sunflower seeds, flax seeds, hemp seeds, and chia seeds. For healthy fats to cook with, choose coconut oil, olive oil, or avocado oil.

6.   6. Mineral supplements: As your diet changes, so does your body's mineral content. To make sure that you're getting enough, please have enough salt in your meals. You can also take mineral supplements if you're concerned, you're not getting enough from your meals.

Now that you know what you can and can't eat with the keto diet, it's time to break it down into some ideas for breakfast, lunch, dinner, and snacks. However, you choose to time your fast, you might only have two large meals in the day, or you might fit in three meals! Remember to choose your meals based on how much you can eat in your eight-hour period without binging. You want to feel full but not overeat.

Keto Breakfast Ideas

For breaking your fast with the keto diet, try to do a combination of eggs, vegetables, meat, and dairy. Here are some possible formulas you can use:

- Eggs + meat + vegetables

- Meat + dairy + vegetables

- Eggs + dairy + vegetables

- Dairy + nuts and seeds + berries

Mix it up a little every day because you don't want to be bored with your meals. You'll also gain better health benefits if you vary what you eat. There are a lot of creative people on the Internet, so look for some keto recipes that you'll enjoy while also maintaining your diet. Remember that you want to ensure your breakfast is filling enough for the morning but also light enough not to cause you some gastric upset. You may have to experiment to get it right.

For your breakfast options, consider all types of eggs. Try them poached, fried in olive oil, or turned into an omelet. If you're thinking an omelet would be a good way to start the day, then try different kinds (e.g., mushroom omelet, spinach and feta, or ham-and-pepper omelet). All of these will give you some variety. Egg scrambles are also a great way to incorporate eggs into your breakfast. Think eggs, bacon, and a variety of vegetables, topped with salsa and goat cheese. All these eggy options are great for breakfast. Here are some others:

- Eggs, bacon, tomatoes
- Cheese omelet with onions, tomatoes, and peppers
- Fried eggs in olive oil, with avocado salsa
- Western omelet with cheese, eggs, ham, peppers, and onions

If eggs aren't your thing, then experiment with yogurt. You want to ensure that you're having enough protein and fat to break your fast with, so consider yogurt mixed with nuts and seeds. Add some fruit like raspberries. Be careful with the fruit you choose, as some of it may have a high glycemic index, which are fruits that can cause a spike in your blood sugar because of their carb content. Here are some yogurt ideas:

- Full-fat, unsweetened yogurt with almonds, chia seeds, and raspberries
- Unsweetened yogurt with peanut butter, cocoa powder, cocoa nibs, and a sugar alternative

If eggs and yogurt aren't for you, then try some other alternatives. You can do chia pudding, which is chia seeds soaked in milk (dairy or non-dairy) with fruit and nuts added to it. There are a lot of options with chia seeds, and they make a delicious creamy pudding.

Keto Lunch Ideas

While fasting, lunch will probably be your biggest meal, so you'll want to make sure you're eating enough to be full. There's no formula for this, so let's just jump right into some possibilities.

Salads are always an option for lunch, but you don't want it to be just vegetables. While a vegetable salad is nice, it's not going to keep you satiated for long. So, if a vegetable salad is what you want, also prepare a snack for later. Your salad can have a base of romaine, spinach, kale, or other leafy greens. Then top with some vegetables. Roasted peppers, olives, tomatoes, cucumbers, and avocado are some options. Top with some nuts, seeds, or cheese for flavor. Then have some meat added. The dressing is the tough part. A lot of condiment dressings from the grocery stores are high in sugar and carbs. You can make your own dressing at home if you want to. You can do this by mixing oil with acid. Think olive oil and lemon juice, balsamic vinegar and olive oil, etc. Here are some salad ideas:

- Spinach, strawberries, goat cheese, chicken, and walnut salad
- Chicken salad with tomatoes, cucumbers, red onions, and feta cheese
- Caprese salad with tomatoes, mozzarella, basil, olive oil, and a side of chicken
- Egg salad with bacon, tomatoes, avocado, and blue cheese
- Spinach salad with shrimp, salsa, lime, avocado, and plain Greek yogurt (sounds strange but so good)
- A mix of greens, topped with tuna salad, tomatoes, and celery
- Arugula cobb salad with boiled eggs, turkey, tomatoes, avocado, bacon, and blue cheese

Sometimes a salad is a boring option for lunch. It's nice to mix it up and try different things for lunch. Here are some complete meal ideas for your lunch:

- Peanut butter milkshake with almond milk, cocoa, peanut butter, ground flax seeds, and protein powder

- Stir-fry with eggplant, beef, peppers, and onions

- Burger patty (no bun!) with cheese, salsa, guacamole, all wrapped in lettuce

- Roasted chicken with cauliflower rice, herbs, cheese, and tomatoes

You don't always have to have a complex meal for lunch. It can be a handful of random things that make a decent lunch or a decent grazing opportunity if that's how you like lunch. If you want some lunch ideas like this, here are a few. Remember, they're not all mixed together. Instead, it is more like a bunch of sides that you happen to eat at the same time. So, for this list, it's just individual ingredients, and you can mix and match them for your lunch. The formula might look something like this: meat + dairy + nuts/seeds + vegetable + treat. Even though these are all small pieces, you want to make sure you pack enough for a robust lunch. You'll be fasting in a couple of hours after eating lunch, so you want to be full, not hungry or hangry.

7.   1. Meats/eggs: Some choices for meat can be slices of turkey, ham, or bacon. Some people like to use salami or pepperoni as well because they're flavorful. You can choose other meats like sausage, roasted chicken pieces, or even meatballs. Smoked salmon is a personal favorite and makes for a delicious lunch. If you don't want to eat meat, you can have two boiled eggs (if you're not already bored with eggs, of course).

8.   2. Dairy: With your pieces of meat, you can have a mix of easy-tohold cheese. This isn't the time to bring a log of goat cheese or a wedge of Gouda. Instead, have some ready-to-eat cheese. Sliced cheddar, Havarti, or provolone from the deli of your grocery store can make an easy addition. Crumbled feta or goat cheese can also work. Other options for cheese include string cheese, cubes of cheese, or even those small Babble cheeses. If you don't want to eat cheese with lunch, consider a cup of yogurt, a glass of milk, or a condiment like tzatziki sauce.

9.   3. Nuts/seeds: These are straightforward. Just choose some nuts that you like and throw a handful into a bag. Almonds, pistachios, or macadamia nuts make good choices.

10. 4. Vegetables: Your vegetable choices can be a variety of things. Just remember to choose lowcarb ones. You can choose one-half of an avocado, slices of cucumbers, grape tomatoes, celery, or slices of peppers. All of those can be raw, but if you want something cooked, consider sautéed zucchini or eggplant. Roasted broccoli, cauliflower, and Brussels sprouts are also top choices. Finally, guacamole and salsa are excellent options as a vegetable side.

11. 5. Treat: A treat is something that's a nice ending to your lunch. Think something sweet or tangy. A handful of blueberries, raspberries, or blackberries make an excellent option. Trail mix with some coconut in it is also a great choice. If you want something more decadent, have some dark chocolate or coconut chips.

Keto Dinner Ideas

Your dinner is going to be the last meal right before you start your fasting period. Because of this, you want to make sure it's well balanced. To include keto with your dinner, you should avoid all the starchy sides most Americans have with dinner. This means no rolls, potatoes, rice, or pasta with your dinner. Dinner is also when you can experiment more with different kinds of fish, which you may not be able to have at work, depending on your work environment. Try to have fish at least once a week for dinner, as it provides you with some good omega-3s and other positive health benefits. Here are some fish dinner options:

- Salmon burgers (without the bun) with a yogurt sauce on a bed of cooked greens
- Salmon filets with buttered asparagus
- Shrimp scampi with zucchini noodles
- Blackened tilapia with guacamole, a bed of leafy greens, salsa, and avocado-lime sauce

You can't have fish for every dinner meal, no matter how tempting it is, so explore some other options. Vary your meat consumption throughout the weeks. With keto, the goal is to have high amounts of protein and healthy fats, so mix it up. You can mix and match your meat with dairy and vegetables. Here are some ideas:

- Meatballs with tomato sauce and cheese, with zucchini noodles

- Stuffed chicken with pesto and feta (served with vegetables)

- Burger with bacon, cheese, egg, and red onion, all wrapped in a lettuce "bun"

- Steak and eggs with a side of cooked spinach • Roasted chicken with mashed cauliflower and herbs

- Steak with cheesy broccoli

- Chicken curry with a side of riced cauliflower and cilantro

- Beef chili (without beans), served with cheese, sour cream, and chives

- Stuffed peppers with ground turkey, mushrooms, and onions, topped with cheese

When choosing to combine keto with your intermittent fast, remember that your meals must be filling and well balanced so that you're not hungry a couple of hours later. Since keto requires you to cut down on carbs, make sure you are carefully counting the carbohydrates you're ingesting.

Fasting with Caloric Restriction

By following a calorie-restricted diet, you're going to reduce how much you eat. You could take all the recommended items from the last two diet sections and eat those, but at reduced serving sizes if you wanted to. You want to keep the same lesson in mind that was repeated in the last two sections: combine protein and fiber to make you feel fuller for longer.

Depending on how many calories you want to eat each day, your meals might vary. To find the best meals for you, I recommend finding and following recipes to the letter. This way, you'll have a very clear idea of how many calories are in each meal. You can also use tracking apps that will tell you how many calories are in how many grams of food. This means that you'll need to measure your food out to know how much you're eating.

When eating your meals, try not to dip below 1,300 calories per day. This is to ensure that you're not falling into malnourishment. If you're worried about not having enough vitamins, then you can bolster your nutrients with supplements if necessary. While following a calorie-restricted diet, you're going to eat mostly fruits and vegetables, lean meats, lowfat dairy, and of course, eggs.

Low-Calorie Breakfast Ideas

With a low-calorie breakfast, you're going to look at eating smaller portions than you would with a full, well-balanced meal. Put some emphasis on foods that don't have many calories but will provide you with a lot of nutrients, like vegetables. These breakfast items are going to be low in calories but mix protein and fiber to keep you fuller for longer. Each of them is less than 400 calories. If they are not filling enough but you want to stick with a lowcalorie breakfast, then add some vegetables. There are many vegetables that are low in calories, and a few fruits too. Add these to your meals to help you feel fuller. Here are some ideas for breakfast:

- Two scrambled eggs on whole-grain toast with asparagus.

- Spinach omelet and low-fat cheese (or goat cheese for flavor), with a slice of toast

- Yogurt, granola, and berries. Depending on how many calories your yogurt has, you can always add seeds like sunflower seeds to your yogurt.

- Fruit-and-yogurt smoothie with flax seeds.

- Oatmeal and yogurt with berries.

- Avocado guacamole on a whole-grain bagel.

Keep a detailed journal about whether these meals help satiate your hunger first thing in the morning. You might want to snack on fruit or vegetables throughout the day if you're feeling like you're still hungry after breaking your fast.

Low-Calorie Lunch Ideas

For lunch, you want to keep up the combination of protein and fiber. You could follow the same lunches as those in the keto diet mentioned above. Just reduce the portions and add more vegetables. If you want some more variety, here are some ideas for low-calorie lunches. Some of these are meals, but many of them are individual components that you just eat all together. All of these are below 400 calories.

- Vietnamese spring rolls filled with vegetables and shrimp: Add a side of peanut sauce, some fruit, and a very small handful of nuts (like ten nuts).

- One slice of whole-wheat bread, two tablespoons of peanut butter, and a banana: All of this together can make that beautiful peanut butter and banana sandwich we mentioned earlier. Add a yogurt cup and a vegetable of choice to round out your meal.

- Two hard-boiled eggs, grape tomatoes, one-half of an avocado, and some crackers: Choose your crackers carefully depending on how many calories you want to eat.

- Three slices of turkey and cheese, one-half of a pita bread, and a side of veggies and fruit to munch on.

A good option for a calorie-light lunch is salads. Just watch what extras you put on them. Many salads at restaurants are way more calories than you would think. If you want a dressing to top it, then make sure that you include the dressing in your calorie count. When making your salad, you have a general formula you can follow to ensure it's low in calories but also filling leafy greens + vegetables + protein + tasty goodness.

• Leafy greens are your typical spinach, romaine, and arugula.

• Vegetables mean slices of plain, regular vegetables: Try not to add anything to the vegetables, as this adds more calories.

• Proteins include lean meats and fish: Consider having half a shredded chicken breast, a handful of shrimps, or two hard-boiled eggs. If you don't want something meaty, then consider beans, crumbled tofu, or roasted chickpeas.

• Tasty goodness: This refers to foods that are delicious and nutritious. What comes to mind is shredded cheddar cheese, sunflowers, walnuts, onehalf of an avocado, or some raisins.

The key to a good salad is one that mixes all of these together without bombing your salad with calories. Again, if you're going to have a dressing, be careful with how much you add and how many calories each teaspoon is. Then calculate that along with your salad ingredients. These salads below are some good options:

• Spinach and arugula salad with strawberries, blueberries, and some sliced almond: Add some crumbled cheese but only after you calculate the calories.

• Mixed greens, one hard-boiled egg, corn kernels, tomatoes, and black beans: Add some salsa for a spicy twist.

Low-Calorie Dinner Ideas

If you had a low-calorie breakfast and a low-calorie lunch, you're probably sitting at roughly 600–800 calories eaten already in the day. This means that you can have dinner with more calories. You can always switch this so that lunch is your biggest meal if you want to. To ensure that your dinner doesn't ruin your calorie goals, make sure the ones you choose have 600 calories depending on what you ate. Of course, all of this depends on how many calories you would like to eat in a day while also keeping in mind the 1,300-calorie malnourishment number. However, these numbers so far place you at 1,200– 1,400 calories in your day with dinner. So, you can choose to eat more if it fits within your calorie goals. Here are some ideas for dinner that are all roughly (depending on your ingredients of choice and portion size) 600 calories:

- Salmon fillet with rice, roasted tomatoes, and pumpkin seeds.

- Meatloaf with broccoli and roasted sweet potatoes.

- Fried rice and chicken with carrots, peas, and chives: Choose the oil you fry in carefully and consider how many calories are in one tablespoon of your oil of choice.

- Roasted chickpea tacos with lettuce, avocado, radishes, lime, corn tortillas, and some Greek yogurt to replace sour cream.

- Crustless quiche with spinach, onions, and bacon (just a little): If you're desperate for the crust, which is the best part, have no meat inside the quiche and add broccoli.

- Lentil and barley soup with slices of grilled chicken, spinach, kale, tomatoes, and lemon.

Low-Calorie Foods to Choose From

Fasting can make you hungry, and if some of these meals are not holding you over, then consider snacking on some items that have very few calories. Here is a list of some foods that have less than 100 calories, are highly nutritious, and will make good snacks without ruining your calorie restriction goals:

- Cucumbers

- Radishes

- Celery

- Carrots

- Bell peppers

- Broccoli

- Clementine's
- Apples
- Strawberries
- Watermelon
- Grapefruit
- Kiwi
- Blueberries
- Low-fat cottage cheese
- Popcorn

Just because these foods are nutritious and have fewer calories does not mean that you should eat them without stopping. Measure out how much you're eating to make sure that you're not eating too much and ruining their caloric goodness. One cup of watermelon is perfect, but one whole watermelon is not. So, measure how much you are eating and still count it toward your daily calorie limits. At this point in the book, you should know when to eat and what to eat while doing intermittent fasting. Choose your foods well, as they are the key to being successful on the fast. If you are going to fast in conjunction with a specific diet, please make sure that you are not depriving yourself of the necessary nutrients your body needs to get through its day. Ensure that you are eating more than 1,300 calories in a day and make sure that all your meals are nutritious. Finally, add variety to your meals because this will give you the best mix of nutrients and vitamins to help you through your fast.

If you want to eat out during your fasting window, keep the protein fiber rule in mind to help ensure your food choices will power you through your fasting period. In the next chapter, we're going to look at how exercise connects with fasting and some of the best ways to approach exercise while on a fast.

Chapter 12

Exercise and Fasting

Exercising is the key to living healthy, and if you're choosing to fast for the same reason, then it makes sense that you'll want to add exercise to your fasting schedule. This isn't a requirement for having a successful fast, but many people already exercise before fasting and want to continue it. Whether you're just starting with exercise or you want to continue your normal workout routine, this chapter will discuss how to incorporate exercise into your new lifestyle.

When to Exercise

Fasting is all about when to eat, even more so than what to eat. The importance of timing is what helps you become the healthiest. So, on that journey to health, the timing of exercise should be taken into consideration. This is a question that many people have when first doing intermittent fasting. Most of us believe that if we don't have food, then we'll end up shaky and weak while we exercise. It's true that some people may feel like this, but there are also some people who are completely fine with exercising without eating first. Let's investigate the different options for when to exercise.

Exercising before You Eat

There are a lot of people who choose to exercise early in the morning before they head to work. Many of them exercise during a fasted state, where they haven't eaten after they woke up. To them, they may feel that they perform better without food in their stomach. But what about if you're fasting for 16 hours before you exercise? Is this a healthy way to exercise? Well, yes and no.

There is a lot of conflicting research and information about whether someone should exercise in a fasted state. In some studies, there were results where people burned more stores of fat. This was more than if they had eaten before fasting. You may burn more fat because there isn't any intake to fuel your workout. So, while your body might normally have recently ingested carbs to burn, when exercising in a fasted state, the body can only use its stores of fat. While this sounds really promising, it doesn't really add anything to your exercise. You're not going to lose more weight or more fat; it's just that your body is using its stores quicker. The benefit that you will receive is better blood sugar levels since you won't have anything ingested to mess with them.

There are some downsides to fasting and exercising without eating. These are not always supported in research, but there is a chance that your body will burn through your muscle protein instead of your fat stores to provide fuel. This means that you'll lose muscle mass as your body uses it to get through the workout. This is obviously negative because it does the exact opposite of what a workout is supposed to do. There's also another negative aspect, which is that exercising on a fast may slow down your metabolism. So, when choosing your exercise time, take into consideration some of these possible rawbacks.

Exercising after You Eat

The other option is to exercise after you eat. A lot of people like to do this because they may feel dizzy or weak if they exercise on an empty stomach. Eating before you exercise has long been proven to be beneficial, especially for athletes who need the energy to keep exercising for hours. Eating a carbheavy meal before you do a long-duration exercise can provide your body with the needed energy and glucose to power your workout without you feeling weak. They'll help strengthen you. However, most of us aren't athletes. So, do we need to eat before we exercise? It just depends on you.

Go with What Makes You Comfortable

The best choice for figuring out your workout times while fasting is to go with whatever makes you feel the most comfortable. As mentioned earlier, some people feel weak if they don't eat before they work out. Some people feel nauseous if they exercise after eating, even after several hours of eating. So, choose the time that works best for you.

The reason why you can choose your own timing is that, through all the research studies on exercising in a fasted or non-fasted state, researchers couldn't find consistent results that showed one was better than the other. The research isn't consistent, and most of them demonstrate no difference between whether you eat before or after you exercise. If you're still not sure which way to go, then break it down like this:

•   If you're going to do a short-duration training or a low-impact exercise, then you don't have to eat before you exercise.

•   If you're going to do a high-duration exercise or a high-impact exercise, then eat three to four hours before you plan on exercising.

Either which way, once you are finished exercising, you should eat something. It doesn't have to be immediately, but it should be as soon as you can. Eating after exercising helps your body recover by giving it the necessary protein and carbs to build up its stores again. If you're exercising right before your eating window, then have a good meal once you are finished. At that point, you would have been without food for 16 hours and would have just used up the last of your stores of energy. So, eat a good meal to help you recover faster.

Exercising on Different Fasting Schedules

Based on which fasting schedule you choose to follow, there are several different options of when to exercise. It's best not to exercise after your last meal in the evening unless you couldn't get it in earlier. While you are transitioning into your fasting schedule, ease up on your normal workout routine. Your body is already going through a change and keeping your same workout (or starting a new one while also starting your fast) may cause you some discomfort. Once you've settled into your fasting schedule, you can start exercising again at your regular level or start a new exercise routine. Here are some ideas for each of the different schedules mentioned in chapter 2.

For the early eating schedule and assuming you wake up at 6:00 a.m., you could exercise between 6:00 a.m. and 7:00 a.m. Since you'll be exercising in a fasted state, work with some exercises that are low impact and in short duration. Consider something like yoga, biking, or walking for less than an hour. You could even do some light weightlifting. After exercising, eat your first meal of the day at 7:00 a.m.

Make sure that your first meal is substantial and has a good mix of protein and fiber.

For the other fasting schedules, you can follow the same information. So, for the midday eating schedule, you could start exercising at 9:00 a.m. and break your fast at 10:00 a.m. For the evening eating schedule, exercise between 3:00 p.m. and 4:00 p.m.

Break your fast at 4:00 p.m. with a meal that is high in protein and fiber.

Here's one final note about exercising in a fasted state: If you're used to exercising in a fasted state, then make sure you take some time to adjust to your new fasting time. It's important to recognize that you've just spent 16 hours fasting, which is significantly different from exercising after eight hours of sleep.

If you want to exercise after eating, then during the early eating schedule, you would exercise three hours after your morning meal or three hours after your midday meal. You'll follow the same pattern for the other eating schedules. Whichever you choose, just make sure that you can eat after you exercise. Don't exercise at the end of your eating window when you can't eat. Since you'll have a meal before you exercise at this time, you can do high-intensity exercise or endurance exercise. This includes things like playing a game of basketball, long-distance running, or HIIT workouts.

Chapter 13
Troubleshooting Difficulties while Fasting

Now that you know all the ins and outs of intermittent fasting with the 16/8 method, everything will go perfectly. Well, in an ideal world, everything would be perfect. But as we know, nothing is so easy. Just like with any goal, especially for improving health, there is a high likelihood that you're going to run into problems. Once you hit a snag, it's easy to want to throw in the towel and just give up. But please don't. When it comes to following a specific eating schedule, it can be difficult, but the rewards are well worth it. So even if you're struggling, try to keep it up. In this chapter, we're going to discuss some areas where you might be struggling and how to rally to keep going.

The Struggle

If you find that you're struggling with maintaining the fast, then there might be several issues happening. You might not be following a schedule that is good for you, or you might have jumped in too fast without giving your body time to adjust. Both things can make it difficult for you to excel at the fast. To help solve this problem, go back to your journal and see what you've done so far. Then change some things up. You could take a break from fasting and restart it, entering the fast slowly. You could also try shifting your eating and fasting windows. You could even reduce how much time you're fasting and just stay at 12 hours of fasting and 12 hours of eating for a couple of months. You could increase to 14 hours of fasting and 10 hours of eating once you are feeling more comfortable. Try different things to see what works best for you. Don't give up until you've tried a couple of different aspects.

Weight Gain

It's one thing to be working so hard on fasting, only to stay at the same weight. To gain weight while fasting can be really disheartening. However, don't take it as a sign that you should just stop fasting. You just need to tweak some aspects of your fast. There are many reasons why you might be gaining weight.

Perhaps you may be eating too much, eating too little, or eating with poor nutrition.

Gaining weight from eating too much is self-explanatory. If you're consuming far more calories than you're using, then you're going to gain weight. When you're fasting, you may be eating more than you need for several reasons. Maybe you're subconsciously worried about going hungry, so to mitigate this problem, you eat a lot more for each of your meals. It's easy to see how this concern might lead to overeating. Instead of eating everything in sight, start paying attention to what you are eating and in what quantities. Keep a food journal or add a food journal to your fasting journal. Record everything you are putting in your body. When keeping a food journal, it can be surprising to see just what we are eating. We might think that all we had was a banana, but after reviewing the journal, we may see that we ate way more than just a banana. If you're someone who is an unconscious eater, someone who eats when stressed or bored, then you'll want to take a more mindful look at how you're eating. We'll discuss mindfulness a bit later in this chapter.

After reviewing your food journal, look for areas you can improve. If you find that you're just eating massive meals, then find ways to cut down on what you're eating. You could replace half of your dish with a salad instead of more pasta, for example. This will help you feel full without ingesting as many calories as you would with a full plate of pasta. If you're worried about going hungry, how about trying to eat reduced portions first, then analyzing how you feel after. Do you feel hungry, or do you feel okay? If you are feeling hungry, then increase the protein and fiber in your meals. This can help calm your hunger hormone and make you feel fuller longer.

Another reason why you might be gaining weight is that you are eating too little. This sounds counterintuitive, but it makes a lot of sense when you understand the human body. When our body feels like we're not getting enough nutrition, it automatically decides that we must be facing famine. This is an evolutionary state where our body takes this environmental information and does everything it can to save us, even when we're not actually facing a famine. In order to save itself, our body starts hoarding everything that we eat and drastically reduces our metabolic rate, and if it's still not enough, it will start cannibalizing our muscles. In a situation like this, you would only lose weight once your body starts focusing on our slightly fewer necessary organs. In that case, you'll have a lot more to worry about than weight gain.

This is a risk if you're doing both fasting and calorie restriction, but it can happen if you are not intentionally controlling your calories. It's very important that you are eating enough—but not too much or too little. You need to have a balanced diet in order to benefit from a fasting state. Just like if you're eating too much, keep a food journal and write down everything you're eating. Include your portion sizes and then analyze where you can make improvements. If you can't figure out where to make improvements, then talk to a nutritionist. They can give you clear guidelines, recipes, and ideas of how you can eat more and take your body out of its starvation state. If you're still eating too little after all of this, it's time to back out of fasting and consider talking to your doctor. There may be something else going on, and your doctor can help you figure it out. The final reason you might be gaining weight while on intermittent fasting is that of poor nutrition. We've talked about the importance of having a balanced diet, but let's assume that you've decided not to follow that recommendation. If you're eating out every day and eating things that are high in unhealthy fats and calories, then you're going to be taking in too many nutrients. You'll gain weight, which is a natural reaction to having a surplus of nutrients. Again, if you think that you're eating healthy, then prove it by keeping a food journal. Honestly, we all think we're eating healthy, but a food journal can show us exactly where we aren't. So long as you are using your journal to analyze your meals and make improvements, you'll gain a lot of benefits from keeping one.

At the end of the day, if you're eating healthy, well-balanced meals and are still gaining weight, then talk to a nutritionist and your doctor. You could be having some other things happening in your body and your doctor/nutritionist can help you solve the mystery.

Keeping a Journal of Progress

This keeps getting harped on throughout this book, so hopefully, by this point you have a journal you're using to track your fast. The journal is awesome for keeping your fasting goals, having a record of your schedule, and tracking the success of your goals and diet. However, it can also be a record of your triggers and lapses.

Triggers are things that made you stop fasting or following your diet. People have different triggers, so it's hard to know for sure what will trigger someone to stop eating right or to stop fasting. Some examples might be a death in the family that causes you to lapse, or it could be a mental health difficulty that reoccurs and causes you to eat more than you should. If you're keeping a journal carefully, then you'll note times when you do not fast or times when you eat too much. When you see this pattern, try to understand what caused it. Was it something that happened that day that changed your mood, or was it something in your life that just made fasting too difficult at that time? Knowing what triggers your decision to stop fasting can help you either avoid it in the future or prepare a plan for when you'll be triggered again.

Lapses are very similar to triggers in that you choose not to follow the fast and stop eating healthily. However, these don't have to have a life event reason. It can just be that you decided to stop. Maybe you were bored, or you wanted to stop fasting over the course of a vacation. You actively choose to stop, so this is a lapse. How you deal with the lapse can help you figure out how to avoid them in the future or how to shift your fast to better fit your plans. All of this and more can be kept in your fasting journal. It can give you a good insight into how you eat and change your relationship with food. In fact, this is one of the benefits that people mention when they talk about intermittent fasting. Having all of this written down gives you a record that you can go back and elaborate on. You can better your understanding about why you eat the way you do and find areas to make improvements. Overall, having a journal can help you overcome some of the difficulties you may have with fasting and eating in general.

Mindfulness

Often when we've gotten into the pattern of fasting or even just regular eating, we do so without thought. This often leads to overeating. It's been mentioned repeatedly in this book that you should eat healthy meals at the right portions. The right portions are those that make you feel full without overeating or undereating. But what does that mean and what does that look like? We often don't recognize our own feeling of satiation until long past our overeating point. We also often miss our hunger cues or misinterpret psychological cues as hunger instead of listening to our body's hunger cues. This can cause us to struggle with our eating habits. To help us overcome this, we need to learn to be mindful about our eating habits and our relationship with food.

Mindfulness is the state of being aware of the present moment. It's about paying close attention to what is happening right now at this moment and allowing wandering thoughts to come and go without passing judgment. When it comes to eating, mindfulness is being aware of what is on the plate in front of us and being aware of our body's response to putting food in our mouth. It might involve paying attention to our five senses as we eat and taking the time to categorize what we're feeling. We might take a moment to understand where we are and what is happening around us. But then we always bring our awareness back to the food we are eating and our body's response.

The goal of mindfulness while eating is all about body awareness and food awareness. As someone who is already fasting, these are things you're already concerned about. Mindfulness goes into more detail about them. With mindfulness, you're learning to pay attention to your body. How does it feel as you are eating a certain item? What does the item look, taste, smell, feel, or even sound like? How does your body feel as the food goes down? And when you're digesting, what are you noticing? Has your energy level spiked or dropped? Is your heart racing or steady? Things like these are a part of mindfulness.

These clues can help you know whether what you're eating is helping or harming your state of being. With mindfulness, you're also learning to recognize when you are physically hungry, not just psychologically hungry.

We can all look at the clock and say, "Man, I haven't eaten for hours! I'm hungry." But are we hungry, or is that just our psychological trigger telling us that we should be hungry? Learning to recognize our true physical hunger signs can help make the fasting process easier. It makes it simpler to know when it's time to eat during the eating window and when it's okay to continue fasting. Mindfulness can also help you know when it's time to stop eating. As we continue practicing mindfulness, you'll start to notice when your body becomes full and you are satiated. When you eat mindfully and slowly, this feeling will come earlier than you expect. This is because we often are too busy with our thoughts and activities while we eat that we miss the signal all too often. So mindful eating can change the way we approach food and change the way we choose to eat. It's a perfect solution to some of the difficulties with fasting. A final aspect of mindfulness to cover is one that can help you as you are breaking your fast. After 16 hours of not eating and perhaps even after exercising on top of that, it's natural for us to feel hungry. We can learn to break our fast in a more mindful manner by starting with easy liquids or broth or something very light before eating a larger meal. This will help our minds come down from its "hungry, eat now!" mentality and move into one where we have the space to choose our foods mindfully. This will help reduce the chances of binging once you end your fasting time.

Once you've practiced mindful eating, make sure you are recording what you have learned. If you've learned that your body really doesn't respond well to cheese, then learn to do without or find alternatives. If through mindfulness you realize that you were overeating before, pay attention to your body while eating and stop when it tells you to stop. Mindfulness throughout the fasting process can guide you to better enjoy your fast and can help you overcome difficulties.

Support Systems

The help that a support system can provide really can't be underestimated. When you're struggling with your fast, reach out to your friends, family, and loved ones. It's important to talk to people who will support you, not the people who will dramatically gasp, clutch their pearls, and scream that you're starving yourself. Talk to people who can help give you the motivation to continue fasting. You can even have friends who can help keep you accountable for following your eating schedule and eating healthy meals. If your friends want to join you while you fast, this is a bonus.

Some of us don't really have friends who can support us. In these cases, turn to social media. There are so many groups on Instagram, Facebook, or Twitter that are all about intermittent fasting. A personal favorite is the intermittent fasting group on Reddit. Their URL is https://www.reddit.com/r/intermittentfasting/. They're so supportive of one another and always post success stories. It's also a great place to get advice if you're struggling with aspects of your fast. You can always find support to help you while you're struggling. You're not alone, so don't give up.

Continue trying with your fasting plan.

Conclusion

You've made it to the end of the book! By this point, you should have learned everything there is to know about the 16/8 method of intermittent fasting. You're ready to start your journey and your transition into fasting. Remember some key things while you fast:

- Always keep a record of your progress.

- Have SMART goals.

- Follow your fasting schedule.

- Eat healthy, well-balanced meals.

- Keep exercising.

- Be mindful about how and when you eat.

- Get some support when you're struggling with your progress.

These tips will help you succeed in your fast. We hope you've enjoyed this book and learned everything you wanted to learn about intermittent fasting and the 16/8 method. Good Luck with your fasting journey!

CPSIA information can be obtained
at www.ICGtesting.com
Printed in the USA
BVHW050904160621
609639BV00005B/1277

9 788659 920191